IMAGINE ME...

A Fiction-Based Novel with Immense Revelation

Anthony D. Walker Jr.

Copyright © 2011 Anthony D. Walker Jr.

All rights reserved. No part of this publication may be reproduced, stored in a retrieval system, or transmitted in any form or by any means, electronic, mechanical, photocopying, recording, or otherwise, without the prior written permission of the publisher.

ISBN: 978-0-615-50724-8

Published by Anthony D. Walker Jr., Wilmington, De

Editing and Layout by L. A. Lambert

Cover Design by Criative Ink

Printed in the United States of America

This book is dedicated to the endless lives of my God brother, **Dorian Tyree Hollman** *& my cousin* **Damond Eugene Gray***. Through my success, your dreams in life will forever be reached. Rest in Paradise.*

Introduction

It was the mid 90's, 10:31 pm on mystery night and I was five years old. Me and Brandon were in the living room eating peanut butter and jelly sandwiches with daddy and mommy.

"Ya'll done eating yet?" Daddy asked as he walked towards the kitchen to throw his food away.

"Yes daddy." Brandon and I said at the same time while laughing together; being a little goofy.

"I think it's time for you little fellas to head up yonder." Mommy stopped us as she pointed to the direction of the stairs so that we could get ready for school in the morning.

As we began moving toward the direction of the steps, me and Brandon raced to mommy and daddy and gave them a kiss on their cheeks. We really didn't want to go to sleep yet because it still felt like morning time, so instead, we quietly turned on our TV while shutting our bedroom door so that mommy or daddy couldn't hear it. We were living the good life, but just like in movies, everything that looks good usually sucks; especially if you're from the place I'm from.

As a kid, I could never imagine my life being a disaster because everything was going right. Well, except for right now because I could tell that something was bothering my mommy by the way she was acting during our family time. Like, every time I tried to think of the worst, I would begin to shake and my nerves would start to act up like old people. I dazed into the television screen, hoping that I would forget about all the bad stuff before tomorrow morning.

The next day at school, my day was going good until I ran into a problem with my teacher, Mr. Gerald. I was in kindergarten and my classroom was room 302. In my class, we were working on arts and crafts that we had to finish by the end of the day before we left school. I was shocked to see all of the newspaper Mr. Gerald put on our tables for our paper Mache's, especially papers with grown up dating advertisements on them. As the other kids in my class continued working on their art, I stopped to raise my hand so that I could ask to use the bathroom. I knew that if I peed on myself I would get in trouble with mommy and daddy when I got back home. Once Mr. Gerald seen my hand raised, he started walking over to me. I guess he thought that I had a question about my art at first, but when I asked him, he told me no. Mr. Gerald said I couldn't go to the bathroom because every day I always seemed to go around the same time. At home, mommy taught me and Brandon to stick to a time when we wanted to use the bathroom while being at school. I didn't want to talk back or get in trouble by Mr. Gerald, so I just obeyed his decision and continued to do my work.

While working on my paper Mache mask, I thought about the Halloween Party that mommy and daddy were taking me and Brandon to at our church tonight. I also thought about the ninja costumes that we were going to be wearing. Mommy told me and Brandon that we were gonna be Holy ninja's for Jesus and that we were gonna be able to fight in God's army because we would be equipped. We both didn't understand what she was talking about, but shook our heads in agreement.

I was so anxious to get out of school because I knew that mommy and daddy would be waiting for me and Brandon at our bus stop. Minutes went by and school was finally over. I rushed out of the class room to get to the bus yard so that I could meet up with Brandon, but he was no where in sight. I wasn't thinking at the time to use the bathroom because I was too excited about getting home so I could put on my costume for the Hallelujah Fest tonight at my church. My brother finally came to the bus yard to meet up with me and we wasted no time heading to our bus to get a seat.

"RJ, mommy said that Aunt Jackie was coming too with Eric and Patrick." Brandon said as he gave me a hug with excitement.

Whenever Brandon got too excited about something, he would give me a hug and start singing tunes from a song as he danced to it. I started to think about Aunt Jackie and the funny things she would do that I would never understand. *Nooo body knows the trouble I see, nobody knows but me!!* Aunt Jackie would sing that song every time she felt that something was about to happen or if something happened already. The funny thing was that each time she sang the song, she would go into her *heavenly language*, screaming and running through out the house with holy oil. Very soon, I would finally realize that Aunt Jackie wasn't so crazy after all.

The bus jerking stopped my day dream and I was brought back to real life. I noticed that our bus trip home from school went by really really fast. I wasn't complaining about it and neither was Brandon because we were too excited about tonight. The bus stopped at the corner of our neighborhood's block to drop us off. We walked in the center aisle up to the front of the bus. Our bus driver, Ms. Trina slammed on the brakes. As she opened the bus doors so that we could get off, Brandon made me trip down the steps. The kids on the bus started laughing and so did me and Brandon. It was a little joke we always played on each other getting off the bus.

The day got really weird once we stepped onto the neighborhood grounds and as we walked, I started to figure out why. Neither mommy nor daddy was at the bus stop to get us. Usually at least mommy would be there, but for some strange reason, we were left alone and unsupervised walking through our neighborhood. That was known as the *usual* though in the kinda environment we were raised in because in the ghetto, everybody was family. Not only that, but being responsible as a kid was something that all of the other kids around our way knew how to be. We finally reached the front door of the house, but before Brandon could twist the door knob, it suddenly opened.

"Brandon and RJ, go straight upstairs!" Aunt Jackie yelled to us while storming back into the dining area of the house.

We were trying to figure out why Aunt Jackie opened the door instead of mommy or daddy, but we were kids as they would say so it didn't matter. I didn't want to get a beating either, so I quickly ran up the steps to the bathroom. I was trying my best to hold it so I wouldn't pee on myself. I almost forgot how bad I had to pee. I lifted up the toilet seat and pulled down my pants fast enough so I didn't have an accident. I woulda really got in trouble then. After that, I went into my room to color, but Brandon didn't. He sat at the top of the steps to ease drop and be nosy. As I colored in my Rugrats coloring book, I could hear screaming and yelling coming from the down stairs. I really didn't pay attention to it until minutes later after I heard loud footsteps coming closer to my room. Daddy opened the door, looking mad with two clothes bags in one hand and Brandon in the other.

"Daddy, where are you taking Brandon?" I asked as Brandon cried and screamed; kicking his shoes off his feet.

"Say good bye to your brother, Brandon." Daddy yelled while sweat ran across his forehead. Not realizing what was happening, I ran behind daddy and Brandon down the stairs.

Before I could run outside to follow them out the house, Aunt Jackie grabbed me by my waist.

"No baby, you can't go out there!" Aunt Jackie screamed while pulling my shirt.

"Why not, where is daddy taking Brandon?" I asked as I began to cry.

"They will be back later so you have to go with me for now." Aunt Jackie insisted as she wiped the tears from my face. "*No... Body knows the trouble I see, nobody knows but me!!*" Aunt Jackie sung as tears built up in her eyes, while holding me tight. "Baby, you're special and God is going to use you and make you spiritually bold to tear down the walls of the devil. The power is in your mouth and the anointing is on your life!" Aunt Jackie cried out, laying her head on my little shoulder. I didn't understand what she was talking about, but before I could ask where my mommy was, I seen that she was stretched out on the floor, further in the back of the dining area by the kitchen.

Chapter One

May 31, 2004

    I couldn't believe that I was graduating junior high school in one week. The class of 2004 was the first graduating class at Downtown Middle School. I was going to miss my school a lot, even the cafeteria ladies. A lot of memories were captured here in the years I had been at this school. The only thing that I wasn't going to miss was the teasing and name calling I experienced from my fellow classmates. I was considered the *church boy* and I was more of an outcast because I didn't get into most of the things my classmates did. I was one who didn't skip school and my teachers could count on me to fill them in on how the class behaved whenever we had a substitute.

    Today had been a good day for me so far, but I grew anxious as I sat in the classroom, watching my teacher write some directions on the board. My mind started to wonder as my insides got happy and for the first time, I was excited to go home after school. My church was having a special service just for the youth and I could only imagine how much fun it was going to be. In the back of my mind, I started to think about the youth activities at church. We did things like face painting, animal crackers, sing-a-long songs like "Father Abraham" and even made animal balloons. This reminded me of how it was like at my old church when Brandon and I went with my mom. Once I moved in with Aunt Jackie, I shared some of my beliefs about church with her. She nipped my imagination in the bud and introduced me to the true importance of church. I never knew what it felt like to catch the *spirit* and I was too curious to find out.

    "Raven Hill, finish your test and stop daydreaming." My teacher Ms. Henry enforced as she tapped my desk.

    I quickly finished up the last few multiple choice questions I had, just as the last bell rang.

"Congratulations students, you've officially completed middle school! I will see you all next week at the graduation rehearsal!" Ms. Henry yelled as students rushed out of the door to get back to the fun part of their lives.

I took my paper up to Ms. Henry and rushed to the front of the building to wait for Aunt Jackie to come and pick me up. As I looked around for her car, I began to think about how much I missed my brother. I hadn't seen him in years and I was sure that he missed me as much as I missed him. After my mom died, the family had split up and communication strings were detached. I heard a familiar horn beeping and looked to see that it was Aunt Jackie pulling up to the side walk.

"RJ get in this car boy." Aunt Jackie smiled, while unlocking the passenger door for me to get inside. "So how was school nephew?" Aunt Jackie asked as I gave her a hug and a kiss on the cheek.

(Now, let me tell you about my Aunt Jackie. Aunt Jackie was one that I could depend on for anything that was going on in my life. She was always the first to know everything and the last to stand when someone challenged her. Aunt Jackie had an interesting way of asking me questions though, but I liked it because it opened up another side of me that I never opened before. Ever since I was younger, she always set high expectations and would speak highly of me to her friends and coworkers. It was like she seen something in me that I didn't see and it would often make me nervous at times because I didn't want her to say anything too deep that I wouldn't understand. Now back to the conversation we were having in the car.)

"It was ok for the most part." I responded back to her. "I can't believe that I'll be in high school next year. Like, I don't think I'm ready for the next step because I don't know what to expect." I dazed out of the window, looking at the birds keeping up with the speed of our car.

"Oh boy, you will be fine as long as you remember to focus and leave those middle school habits in middle school." Aunt Jackie chuckled as she looked over at me. "It's a major transition, but I know for sure you're ready."

Taking in the last bit of what Aunt Jackie was saying, I remembered that today marked seven years since my mom had passed.

"It looks like we'll be going to visit your mother's grave site tomorrow since we have no time today." Aunt Jackie added, just as she stopped at the red light.

"That's fine with me Aunt Jackie." I really didn't feel like going anyway.

Ten minutes later, we pulled up in front of our town house. Me and Aunt Jackie moved after the tragedy of my mom's death and after my dad took Brandon away. She said that she didn't want any memories to haunt her and I for darn sure didn't want anything creeping me out either. I often laughed at Aunt Jackie though because she could be very dramatic and extremely deep when she wanted to be.

Aunt Jackie opened the door and picked up the mail that was lying on the floor. I went to the kitchen to warm up the left over lasagna we had last night once I put my back pack on the couch. I seen Aunt Jackie pick up the house phone to make a call to my older cousin Veronica while looking surprised at the mail she had in her hands. Together, Aunt Jackie and Cousin Veronica are trouble. I love my aunt because although she had a spiritual side that I always appreciated, Cousin Veronica was one who could easily open Aunt Jackie's ghetto side just as fast.

Ever since I was younger, I grew up to know that Aunt Jackie was a fighter and a protector when it came to close people she cared for. I'm not talking about fighting over anything petty either. She would normally give people the benefit of the doubt and would usually ask questions before getting in their grill. Cousin Veronica was the same way, except she had a twist to her. She would hit one first and ask questions later.

"V Baby, V Baby, hey love what you doing?" Aunt Jackie started laughing as she released her hair from the tight rubber band that was holding it into a ponytail. "Girl, tell me why I got some notification letter from the police department..." Aunt Jackie started going up the stairs to finish her conversation with Cousin Veronica.

My mind began to wonder and what I had in mind would be locked in my brain for the rest of the day. I knew that Aunt Jackie may have been in some trouble, but I wasn't sure how much trouble she was in. While sitting at the kitchen table, I heard the door bell ring.

"RJ, who's at the door?" Aunt Jackie yelled from upstairs. I went to open the door and standing on the other side of the door was Lil Rodney.

Lil Rodney is a kid from my neighborhood who got into everything. He was always causing trouble with the people in my neighborhood. He normally would plot on who he wanted to mess with though, but I never seen that side of him before. He's a little older than I am by six months and was very mature for his age just like I was. Lil Rodney respected my Aunt Jackie so much though; he even went so far as to tell her that real recognized real.

"Sup boy, can I come in for a second?"

Lil Rodney dapped it up with me while texting in his cell. I let him inside and just as he entered, I heard Aunt Jackie coming back down the stairs.

"Well if it ain't ole Rodney King!" Aunt Jackie said while laughing.

Aunt Jackie had a sense of humor that made the younger kids love her tremendously.

"Nah Aunt Jackie, it's the other way around." Lil Rodney said chuckling; while giving Aunt Jackie a hug.

I went back to the kitchen to wash my plate, but I knew that Lil Rodney had something up his sleeve. He was the type of person you would normally see around the neighborhood, but would continue to go about your business because you knew it was Lil Rodney. You know when people like Lil Rodney start to come around, I question them. As I walked back into the family room, I saw that Aunt Jackie was in the room alone.

"Aunt Jackie, where did Lil Rodney go and what did he want?" I was curious to know.

"Oh nothing baby, he gave me an invitation to his graduation and his party." Aunt Jackie continued talking. "I didn't know he was graduating and going to high school like you." Aunt Jackie seemed so impressed. "If you see him in your school, tell those kids to runnnnnn." she said as we laughed together.

"Trust me auntie, I'm on it!" We both started laughing again.

"You are a mess RJ, now you know we have to get ready for service soon so go pick out your clothes and lay them on the ironing board so I can iron them." Aunt Jackie got up and walked to the kitchen.

When it came to church, Aunt Jackie gave me freedom to dress how I wanted because I was starting to become a teenager. She didn't just let me wear anything though, but she did embrace my style. The way I dressed was different as she would say because kids my age didn't dress like me. I had a trendier look when it came to my church clothes. Aunt Jackie always warned me though to be careful with my concepts and watch out for those funny *spirits;* and I knew just what she meant by that. As I went up stairs to get my clothes out for Aunt Jackie to iron them, I laughed at the joke she made about Lil Rodney.

About three hours later, we were just about ready to leave for the youth service. Aunt Jackie loved to dress as well and the makeup she wore was unbelievably creative.

"You ready nephew?" Aunt Jackie asked while transporting things from her regular purse to a fancier purse.

"I'm ready auntie." I had my bible in my left hand and a bottle of water in my right hand. It was very rare that a kid my age carried a bible around like I did. I'm talking about to school, through the neighborhood and even throughout the house. Even some of the kids at church thought I was weird for doing that. I didn't care because I knew that I was different and as Aunt Jackie always said, I had what it took for the next generation.

We walked out of the house to get in our car. Within minutes, we finally arrived at church and as we walked in the doors, the praise team was singing. Praise and worship was known to be the tone setter for the rest of the service in church. The service would usually start with praise and worship so that we could usher in the *spirit* as some would say.

"People from every nation and tongue, from generation to generation, we worship you hallelujah, hallelujah…" The praise team sang as people in the audience blew their whistles and clapped their hands.

It only took 30 minutes into the service before church was filled with people. Services like these always drew a crowd because every time a preacher who wasn't from the area came, more visitors seemed to show up. While Aunt Jackie and I were walking in the service to get a seat, Aunt Jackie told me that whatever happened in service tonight, not to be afraid and to go with the *spirit*. My stomach began to get butterflies just as we took our seats. After the praise team was done singing their songs, the Mistress of Ceremonies came to the podium to take over the service.

Ms. Robin was extremely hype and it scared me because I didn't want her to call me out, not that she would anyway. My youth choir had to sing and I had to lead the song that we were singing. "*He woke me up this morning and he started me on my way.... I have food to eat and shoes on my feet and he let me see another day.... Thank you for being so good, yeahhhh!*" More and more people stood to their feet as I continued singing. I don't know what it is, but every time I sang in church, I felt so comfortable and free. We ended the song and went back to our seats. I felt so good because on my way to sit down, all the faces looking at me would be smiling.

Moments later, the service started moving at a fast pace and it was time for the guest preacher to do his thing. I was scared to look at the man because his demeanor wasn't inviting. He just sat in his chair with a serious look on his face. Every time somebody on the program acknowledged him, he would respond with a blank stare, nodding his head saying, bless you. I will say that his long dark denim robe caught my attention instantly though. As I watched him walking up to the podium, he scoped the congregation out, then released a loud scream into the microphone. He almost acted the same way the MC did and it started to make me nervous because I didn't think I was ready for it. The MC couldn't call me out, but I knew that the preacher had the freedom to do so. As a child, I didn't understand everything he was saying, but I knew that he had the audience's attention. Just before he got done preaching, he called all of the kids to the altar so that he could pray with us.

"Now, I know that this is a youth service and I know that some of you don't know what it feels like to let the Lord have his way, but on a count of three I want you all to start leaping. Listen now, I don't want you babies to stop until you feel something." Pastor Pope declared as he called the ministers and other preachers to come up to the altar with us.

There was a few of my friends and some other kids my age standing altogether at the alter. I tried really hard to focus and grasp what was going on at this very moment. Mixed emotions started taking over in my mind, so by the time I finally understood what was about to happen, it was too late. Although I was scared for my life, I knew that the preacher wasn't gonna hurt me because Aunt Jackie would probably kill him.

"One... Two... Three now leap, leap, leap!" Pastor Pope screamed as praise music came on. I continued to leap as the minister's yelled in my face, speaking in tongues and patting my back. As I leaped, something took over me, causing my feet to move in rotation and my arms to flap. I knew after it hit me that it was the *Holy Spirit*. During the time of my dance, I imagined God protecting me and Brandon in his big hands. Tears kept running down my face as I continued to scream from my lungs. I reacted so crazily that one of the ushers had to walk me back to my seat. I was completely focused on God and didn't care what was going on around me.

Just as I got to my seat, I broke out in a dance again and went into another spiritual realm. I'm telling you, it was an uncontrollable feeling that I had no control over. As I calmed down, I heard the guest preacher, Pastor Pope call the parents and guardians up to the altar. He prayed with them and gave them the same instructions, just as he did with us. When he released them, I noticed Aunt Jackie instantly going off and I just watched her. I enjoyed watching Aunt Jackie dance because she jumped so high to the ceiling, almost touching the chandelier. My foot hit something on the floor as I stood with my hands clasped rocking back and forth. I noticed it was Aunt Jackie's bible on the floor with other important papers she kept in her bible. Aunt Jackie sure did hold a lot of papers in her bible, like it was a folder or something. As I picked up the bible and the rest of the papers from the floor, I seen the notification letter that Aunt Jackie was talking to Cousin Veronica about on the phone. I began to read the letter to myself: *'This letter serves to verify to the defendant Jackie Jones, that the plaintiff, Brandon Z. Hill will be released from prison in two weeks...'* I instantly put the letter back into the bible; the way it was and continued to watch Aunt Jackie dancing with tears in her eyes. All of these years had gone by without me knowing where my dad or Brandon was. I wonder why my dad is in jail and where little Brandon is. I knew that Aunt Jackie had to know these things, but wouldn't tell me because I was just a kid. I had to figure out a way to find out exactly what was going on.

Chapter Two

June 11, 2004

It's the day of my graduation from middle school. It started to kick in that I was no longer a middle school student. As I stood in a single file line in the hallway with the graduating class, I began to get nervous. I was on the program to sing the farewell song to the teacher's and my fellow students. I knew that if my mother was here, she would have been proud of me. As I continued standing in line, humming the song I was going to sing, I noticed Aunt Jackie and three kids with her. Once she got closer to the line that I was in, a smile started to form on my face.

"Oh my Lord, look at you!" Aunt Jackie said being the dramatic person that she is.

She had her god kids with her; Kailyn, Eric and Patrick. Eric and Patrick were twins and were my age. Kailyn was a lot younger than us. Me and the twins didn't get a chance to really hang out, except for when we were younger, so we had to catch up on all of the good times. When we were younger, every time Eric and Patrick would come around, it would take a while for us all to warm up and play with each other. It's good to reflect on those moments, especially now because we were moving on to bigger and more mature things in life.

"Mom, can we take a picture with RJ?" Eric and Patrick asked Aunt Jackie as they walked over to my line.

After taking the picture, they rushed into the auditorium

before the ceremony started. I was starting to get anxious because I knew that I had support waiting on the inside of the auditorium.

"All rise and welcome Downtown Middle's graduating class of 2004." I could hear the principal saying over the podium through the loud speakers.

The music began to play and the line started to move. While walking onto the platform to take our seats, I could see Aunt Jackie and my cousins yelling and cheering for me. The ceremony was about to come to a close; which meant it was finally time for me to sing the farewell song to my school.

"At this time we will have a special musical selection by graduating student, Raven Hill." One of my peers introduced me after reading a poem from our class to the teachers. As I stood to my feet, I could hear Aunt Jackie screaming my name, making me even more nervous to sing in front of the unfamiliar faces. While looking out to the audience as I sung, I noticed a parent crying which caused tears to fall from my face. I started to choke up after the first verse. That was the most emotional part of the entire ceremony, at least I thought. My principal, Mr. Warren slowly walked up to the podium after I sat down and gave his final words to the graduating class. I drifted away from what it was that he was saying because I got side tracked by Aunt Jackie nodding off in her seat. This was something new that I never seen before. I always knew Aunt Jackie to be one to have herself together at all times, especially in public.

"She probably didn't get any sleep." A girl named Cambria whispered to me. Cambria was a nosy girl who always wanted to know everything and be a part of everything.

"No, Mr. Warren is just talking too much." I said in response, taking up for Aunt Jackie's actions.

Something strange was up and I didn't have a clue what it was. After throwing up our caps in the air and recessing to the back, I rushed to meet up with Aunt Jackie. Her falling asleep made me feel uneasy and distracted me from being excited about my graduation. I didn't care to take any more pictures, nor did I care to speak to anyone else who tried to get my attention.

"RJ baby, I'm so proud of you." I could hear a voice coming from the crowd of people. I couldn't identify who it was, but I knew that the voice sounded really familiar. It was Cousin Veronica with her two kids. Once I noticed who it was, I went over to give Cousin Veronica a hug and speak to my other cousins, Jay and Asia. I don't know what it is about my cousin Jay, but I always feel uncomfortable every time I'm around him. He makes me feel like I owe him something or I'm beneath him. Aunt Jackie would always say that Jay was a jealous little boy and that he had low self esteem, which was why he always made nasty comments. I really didn't pay him any mind as I spoke because my focus was getting to Aunt Jackie so that we could leave.

After graduation, Aunt Jackie took me and everyone else to Golden Corral, an all you can eat buffet restaurant. Once we arrived there, I sat at one end of the table and Aunt Jackie sat at the other end with Cousin Veronica and her kids. I was happy that Eric and Patrick were here with me because things would have been awkward without them.

"So what school are you going to next year?" Eric asked me while taking a sip of his lemonade.

"Downtown High." I replied while noticing the disappointed look on Eric and Patrick's face.

"Dag, my mom told us that we couldn't go there because it was in the middle of the city and that trouble would be waiting for us at the front door of the school." Eric said.

I laughed uncontrollably while standing up to go to the buffet line. I could see Aunt Jackie and Cousin Veronica talking in my peripheral and it looked like it was about something serious. I wonder if it was about what ever was making Aunt Jackie loose sleep. I didn't want to seem nosey though, so I just kept walking towards the food line, reaching for a plate once I got to it.

"Did ya'll see Aunt Jackie nodding off at the graduation?" I asked just to see if Eric and Patrick noticed.

"I didn't see her..." Eric said.

"But I did." Patrick said, cutting Eric off.

"I never seen auntie do that before because she would always tell me that she had a reputation to uphold." I glanced back over to Aunt Jackie as she continued talking to Cousin Veronica.

"I don't know RJ, but the weirdest thing happened on the way to your graduation." Eric said as he reached for the gravy for his mashed potatoes.

"What happened?"

"Ok, so first of all no music was playing in the car because God mom wanted to be in concert." Eric said laughing.

"Eric, chill cause she was serious as she sang and it was like she kept repeating the same line over and over and over again." Patrick said as he waited for Eric to get done with the gravy.

"Well what song was it?" I asked as if I already didn't know what song she was singing.

"It was something like, 'No... Body knows the trouble I see, nobody knows but me'..." Eric sung as he waited for me and Patrick to get our food.

Once he sung that line, it was confirmation to me that something had been bothering Aunt Jackie. I tried to put the pieces of the puzzle together. One, Aunt Jackie was nodding off, which meant that she was losing sleep and two, she had been singing that song.

While walking back to the table with plates full of food in our hands, Aunt Jackie and Cousin Veronica stood to their feet to get their plates. All that I kept thinking about from that point on was the infamous song Aunt Jackie sung.

"RJ, so what's gonna' be your next step?" Jay asked from the other end of the table, like he wasn't ease dropping on the conversation I already had with Eric and Patrick. He really knows how to get under my skin.

"I'm going to Downtown High." I said with a nonchalant attitude. I didn't hesitate to answer his question.

"My mom would never allow me to go there." Jay said as he went back in his phone to continue his text message conversation.

I didn't even bother to respond to his last statement because Aunt Jackie always told me that every statement didn't require a response. From the time we got to the restaurant up until now, I knew that I had put Jay in an awkward situation because I really wasn't paying any attention to him. As I noticed Aunt Jackie and Cousin Veronica walking back to the table, I started to get butterflies because I knew that something was on Aunt Jackie's mind. She tried to play off how she was feeling with a fake smile.

"Kids is the food good?" Aunt Jackie said as she placed her plate on the table.

"Yes." Everyone said altogether.

I dazed into my own world while eating as my mind started processing everything. Why did all of these years pass without Aunt Jackie having a husband and kids? "Heaven only knows..." I said out loud as my mind joined the table again.

"Heaven only knows what?" Cousin Veronica asked as she looked to Aunt Jackie, as if I had heard their conversation.

"Oh nothing." I hope I didn't dig a hole for myself. "I was just thinking about something that happened at the graduation today."

Aunt Jackie always knew when I was either lying or bothered by something because of the look she often gave me. She would stare while squinting her eyes at me.

A whole hour had passed and we were finally on our way home. I still carried Aunt Jackie's mysterious tendencies in the back of my mind. While dropping Eric, Kailyn and Patrick off, my thoughts got even heavier. I tried my best not to completely zone out because I knew Aunt Jackie would be talking to me in the car on the way back home. But I ended up not paying her any attention because my mind was elsewhere. Aunt Jackie's phone started ringing and I could tell that she was a little hesitant to pick it up.

"Hello." Aunt Jackie answered as she pulled up to the driveway of our home.

I guess it was one of the men from the church because she put on her churchy, Jesus saves, voice. I'm telling you, Aunt Jackie sure did know how to do things and it was funny to me.

While walking up to our house, a police car was parked outside of Lil Rodney's house.

"That boy must've done something." Aunt Jackie said while hanging up her phone with a weird smile.

Once we got inside of the house, there was mail on the floor. As I turned on the light, Aunt Jackie picked up the mail.

About the same time she gathered the envelopes into a stack in her hands, I noticed a blank envelope with my name on it. A startled look came across Aunt Jackie's face as she pulled a wad of cash from the envelope. I counted in my head as Aunt Jackie slowly went through the bills. It was five hundred dollars. She took out the note included with the money and read it to herself.

"This money seems to be for you from your cousin Ray on your dad's side of the family." Aunt Jackie's look changed from startled to skeptical.

Ray was a long lost cousin. It was extremely odd that he would give me money because we never had a close relationship. He was 19 years old and would often hang out with Lil Rodney at times, but other times would do his own thing. I still don't understand their relationship to this day. I wondered if Ray knew what was going on with my dad or even my brother, Brandon. Aunt Jackie put the money back into the envelope and closed the door, looking a bit irritated.

"Stay here RJ." Aunt Jackie said sternly as she re-opened the front door. "I'll be back. I'm going over to Lil Rodney's to see if he's heard from Ray."

Aunt Jackie was not playing because she slammed the door kind of hard behind her. I looked out the window as I watched her cross the street to Lil Rodney's house. Just as I watched Aunt Jackie from the window, I remembered something. I ran up the stairs to my bedroom. Today was Friday and I assumed my dad was getting out of jail this upcoming Monday. The letter I read in church must've been a two weeks' notice; with this being the second week. It was clear to me that those were possible reasons as to why Aunt Jackie had been acting strange.

Chapter Three

June 14, 2004

    Today is the day that my dad is supposed to be released from jail. I have mixed feelings today, feeling happy, yet very nervous. I missed having my dad around, but I knew that Aunt Jackie probably wouldn't let him see me again because of what happened the day he left with Brandon. I really don't think my dad had anything to do with my mom being stretched out on the floor though. In my opinion, I think that there is a little more to the story than what Aunt Jackie has been telling me. Aunt Jackie always found a way to cover things up, especially when it comes to me and Brandon.

    Here I was, 13 years old; still confused about my dad's arrest and my family issues. A lot of questions started popping up in my head as I sat up in the bed. Why in the world would Aunt Jackie over react about this entire situation and who was taking care of my brother while my dad was in jail? All that I could remember was my dad taking Brandon away from me, Aunt Jackie shaking uncontrollably and my mom stretched out on the floor. Tears started to build up in my eyes, slowly pouring onto my face.

    "Before I even knew who I was or what my mom and daddy meant to me." I started singing, just to erase all negative thoughts I had in my tiny little brain. Singing always seemed to calm me down and give me a peace of mind.

It was 11 o' clock in the morning and Aunt Jackie was at work as usual. I was surprised that she even went into work, especially on this mysterious day. I was even more surprised that she allowed me to stay home all by myself.

I got up to wash my face and brush my teeth and noticed Aunt Jackie's door completely shut. That was strange to me because Aunt Jackie never shuts her door, not even when she's here. I quickly brushed my teeth and washed my face, rushing so that I can open Aunt Jackie's bedroom door.

(Let's get this straight, I'm not nosy, but you know how it is when you're alone in a house and you want to inspect every part of the house. Let's just say, I am just that kind of kid and to be honest, it definitely pays off.)

As I opened Aunt Jackie's door, I noticed a man sleeping on her bed. Without even thinking twice, I immediately rushed to my room quietly, calling Aunt Jackie. My heart felt like it was about to come straight out of my mouth and my stomach dropped like I had been on a roller coaster.

"Aunt Jackie, there is a man in your bed." I started talking as soon as I heard her pick up the phone. I didn't even give Aunt Jackie a chance to say hello.

"RJ, its Mr. Marvin from the church!" Aunt Jackie started chuckling. "Now you know I wasn't going to leave you home alone because I don't play that." I could hear Aunt Jackie munching on food. I didn't even bother asking her what he was here for because I knew that Aunt Jackie probably would tell me to stay in a child's place, plus she was a free agent, as she would call it.

"Mr. Marvin will be watching you, just until I get off of work, so try not to bother him." Aunt Jackie sure was something else. "And if you decide to do anything or go anywhere, which I highly doubt, let him know".

It was like Aunt Jackie was telling me things that I already had the common sense to do. "Ok auntie." I said while making my bed.

"Oh yeah and we gotta' talk when I get home so I hope you don't have any plans tonight." Aunt Jackie started laughing again.

"Ok." I began to chuckle to hide my fear. We ended the conversation and I walked back towards Aunt Jackie's bedroom.

Just as I opened Aunt Jackie's door, I noticed Mr. Marvin

sitting at the foot of the bed.

"What's up RJ?" Mr. Marvin started smiling in a weird way.

I could tell that he had a good sleep though because his voice was freshly scratched and he had heavy coal particles in the corners of his eyes.

"Nothing much Mr. Marvin." I was still confused about him being at my house.

"Your Aunt went to work and I'm going to be here with you until she gets off." Mr. Marvin started rubbing his crust stained eyes.

"That's cool with me." I said as I shrugged my shoulders, turning around to walk out of the room. I walked toward the steps so I could get a bowl of cereal from the kitchen.

"RJ, how about a ride through the city?" Mr. Marvin asked as his voice traveled with me down the stairs.

Mr. Marvin was the type of man that everybody loved because he had a personality that was full of life, plus he was outgoing. He knew a lot of people and was very humble when it came to helping them. The only thing was that a lot of women from my church would try to throw themselves at him because he had money. I never really spent time with him outside of church, so this was the first time I really could get to know Mr. Marvin. From what I could tell so far, he was a great person.

"Ok!" I yelled back up the steps excitedly. Even though it was noon and I hadn't eaten anything yet, I forgot about being hungry and my bowl of cereal. I rushed back up the stairs to get dressed.

Aunt Jackie's 1999 Ford Focus was nothing compared to Mr. Marvin's car. He had the new 2004 s500 Mercedes Benz convertible with TV screens installed in the head rest of the seats. We finally arrived in town, making our first pit stop Best Buy. I didn't ask any questions because I was too busy admiring Mr. Marvin's car.

"I told your Aunt that I was getting you a laptop for school." Mr. Marvin started pulling out 100 dollar bills from his arm rest.

"Oh wow, thanks!" That was all I could say because I was speechless. Mr. Marvin was cool with me and definitely had my approval; regarding Aunt Jackie.

We walked in the store and it was like God himself

introduced me to a place that I had never been to before. One of the store clerks walked us over to the computer section of the store. I felt like it was my birthday, even though it was just a graduation present. After Mr. Marvin made the purchase, I could not stop thanking him. I would probably say that I thanked him all the way back to the car.

"Thanks again Mr. Marvin." I said for the hundredth time as I put my seatbelt on.

"No problem man", Mr. Marvin pulled out of the parking spot, smiling with a look of accomplishment on his face. "I don't mind doing things for kids who have their heads on straight and want to make it in life." He added.

I was so excited to get back to the house and play with my new toy. I didn't know everything about laptops, but I knew that it wouldn't take me long to figure it out. I started thinking about why Aunt Jackie was so comfortable with Mr. Marvin staying with me today. I wonder how long Aunt Jackie and Mr. Marvin been messing around; I guess it doesn't matter as long as he keeps us both happy!

Mr. Marvin drove us to McDonalds and brought us lunch before going back home. I guess Mr. Marvin is exactly what Aunt Jackie needs because he is definitely a provider. I could also tell that Aunt Jackie was conversing with Mr. Marvin about what was going on in our family because he started making conversation at random times about some stuff.

After leaving McDonalds, we jumped back on the highway with the sun roof down, cruising on I95. Mr. Marvin must have been into gospel rap music hard because he played A.P.O.S.T.L.E hit song, *Jump* all the way to the house. The beat was hot and before I knew it, we were both rocking and screaming, JUMP.

Minutes later as we pulled into the development, we noticed Lil Rodney and my cousin Ray sitting on my steps. I was so confused as to why they were sitting on the steps.

"I see that your little friends were waiting for you to get home." Mr. Marvin pulled into our driveway laughing.

I didn't want to draw attention to the fear I started developing because I didn't want Mr. Marvin to get any bad vibes from Lil Rodney or Ray.

"Wassup RJ?" Lil Rodney and Ray said at the same time. They stared Mr. Marvin down as he walked into the house with the laptop in his hands.

"Wassup." I was nervous to sit on the steps next to these knucklе heads.

"Cousin, you know ya' dad out." Ray said as if he'd been anticipating getting it out.

"Oh is that right?" I tried playing it off.

"Hell yeah nigga, we heard a lot about him cousin and we just wanna' fill you in." Ray looked over to Lil Rodney. Because I was vulnerable and naive to information regarding my family, I wanted to take it all in.

"Ok." I started getting excited on the inside and I didn't know why. It was kind of weird though because Aunt Jackie really didn't want me to be around Lil Rodney or Ray since she knew that they were skeptical boys; she wasn't home so I didn't care.

"Iight, so word has it that ya' pops got locked up because of what he did to ya' brother". As Lil Rodney and Ray started telling me stuff, nothing was making sense to me.

"Well, what exactly did my dad do to him?" I started thinking about Brandon and how much my dad would yell at him.

"Well, Cousin Eunice, our great cousin told me that ya Aunt Jackie purposely reported abuse to the cops and supposedly gave them pictures she took of little Brandon with scars."

I could tell that Ray was serious. For the first time, my virgin ears were being corrupted by gossip, but I nervously wanted to know more.

"Wait, so why didn't Aunt Jackie keep Brandon and how did my mom die?" I started asking Ray everything, hoping he had the answers.

"Oh, I don't know about all of that, but I just wanted to give you some insight on what's going on around you cousin." Ray patted me on my head as he and Lil Rodney made their way back across the street to Lil Rodney's house.

I was left standing outside, looking stupid because I never thought that things were that deep around me. I really wanted to cry so badly, but I knew that I couldn't go back inside like that because Mr. Marvin would probably question me.

I was finally starting to realize why Aunt Jackie handled me the way she did, especially when she would tell me that nothing was going to ever happen to me. My mind started to wonder as I thought about Brandon and where he was. I wonder how he felt and exactly what it was that my dad did to him. I could feel anger developing in my stomach and that wasn't a feeling I ever experienced before. I was always kept from gossip because my mom always hated it. She always said that the person sharing news was just like an encyclopedia, giving their own interpretations of a story. I started to think some more and that's probably what Aunt Jackie wanted to talk to me about when she got home from work. As I walked into the house with Mr. Marvin, I watched him install games and other software onto my new laptop.

Three hours passed and Aunt Jackie was expected to come through the door any minute from work. I began to get anxious for her to get here because I wanted to know what she had to say to me. Just as I started reading my bible, I could hear Aunt Jackie pulling up into the driveway. I knew that whatever it was Aunt Jackie had to say to me, it was going to be serious because I know my aunt very well. As I heard the front door opening, I rushed downstairs to meet Aunt Jackie. Mr. Marvin was on the couch watching TV when I got to the last step. Aunt Jackie walked in, looking worn and stressed while telling me to meet her up stairs so that we could talk. I could feel butterflies hatching from their cocoon in my stomach as I waited patiently for Aunt Jackie in her bedroom.
As I waited for Aunt Jackie, I could hear Mr. Marvin telling her about Lil Rodney and Ray sitting on the steps of our house. I heard Aunt Jackie's loud footsteps coming closer and closer to her bedroom door and that's when reality hit. She took off her shoes and threw her pocketbook on the ground, sitting on the bed.
"RJ, I really feel as though you are becoming a young man and as you enter high school you are going to be faced with new experiences and conflicts. With that being said, I have to make you aware of some things I have not shared with you before." Aunt Jackie looked troubled. I didn't bother to interrupt her because I wanted to hear what it was that she had to say. "Your father was released from prison today and now he is a free man." I could tell that Aunt Jackie was crying all day as more tears hit her cheeks. Knowing that Aunt Jackie could be dramatic at times, I asked her

why was he in jail and she continued the conversation.

"Well RJ, your dad was very mean to Brandon and was sent to jail once little Brandon ran away and told the nearest person, who then reported abuse. The state took your brother away and now because your dad lost the custody of Brandon, he is in search of you because I guess he feels like he owes it to you." Somebody had the story mixed up because Ray said that Aunt Jackie was the one who reported the abuse.

"But Aunt Jackie, why me?" I don't want my dad taking me away like he did Brandon.

"Apparently, little Brandon is not your biological brother. He was adopted by your mother and father after his real parents neglected and ran out on him.

I started thinking a little more as Aunt Jackie continued talking while heavy tears soaked her face.

"So how did my mom die the day Brandon and I came home from school and why did my dad take Brandon instead of me if I'm his son?" I asked these questions while Aunt Jackie blew her nose.

"Well, that day was crazy because it was already too much going on, but your mom had a seizure that later turned into a heart attack. Seizures run heavily on our side of the family. By the time ya' mom fell out, your dad had already rushed out the door with Brandon. He wanted to take you as well, but your mother would not let him." Aunt Jackie was spilling all of the beans while crying even more. "That lowlife bastard will not get anywhere near you and I promise you that!" Aunt Jackie grabbed me to give me a hug.

"I'm going to let Mr. Marvin know what is going on and see if he could stay with us for a few more days if that's fine with you."

I couldn't believe that my dad put my family in so much pain and I was even more scared to find out what was going to happen next.

"Aunt Jackie, how do you know that my dad is looking for me?" I asked, trying to clear my throat.

"I was granted custody after your mom died. Since your dad was in jail, the court automatically gave me rights over you. But I started hearing that he had a group of boys who were once in jail with him, looking for me so that he could get to you. Now I don't know how true that is, but I just stay alert at all times." Aunt Jackie said as she watched me crying in her arms.

"Auntie, don't let him take me." I repeated to her through my tears.

"Oh trust me, I will do everything in my power to take care of this and that's why I tell you to watch your Cousin Ray because I think he has something to do with this." Aunt Jackie started cursing.

Although Aunt Jackie had her own feelings about Ray, I wouldn't expect Ray to have anything to do with this matter. If anything, he seemed surprised earlier when he told me about my dad, but like I was taught a long time ago, you never know people's true motives.

Chapter Four

February, 2008

Some years had passed and I was now in the middle of my senior year of high school. It amazes me everyday how fast time flies by, yet still I have a photographic memory of the experiences from each year of high school up to my senior year. I could remember everything about my childhood like it was yesterday, from the beatings that I got from Aunt Jackie, even to the most horrific thoughts of my mother's death.

My Aunt Jackie and Mr. Marvin finally got married back in June of 2006 and had a little girl named Jamie last February. Things seemed to be going pretty well with my family and I could now see past all previous hurts and pain. I haven't heard anything about my dad or Brandon from anyone. I've been learning how to release stress and problems that were built up from childhood. I also started applying for colleges away from home because I feel like I need to change my environment. It often gets boring seeing the same stuff every single day, especially around here.

This morning, I was sitting in 1st period class, which was study hall. It felt so good to have study hall as my first class of the day because all of the other years, I had it as my last class of the day. It's too early in the morning to hear lecture's from teachers. Just thinking about college and the freedom that came with it had my insides excited. I thought about different organizations and Greeks that Mr. Marvin would tell me about. Mr. Marvin set up appointments for me to visit Pender's State University, Aponte's Art Institute and Virginia State University. Aunt Jackie gave me money for application fees and she also helped with the essay part on the applications. My grades were pretty good and my GPA was acceptable, I guess.

"RJ, stop wasting time and get back to work." Ms. Howard embarrassed me in front of the entire class. Well, it really wasn't an embarrassment because everybody was doing their own thing, as expected in study hall. It just felt that way to me.

"Ms. Howard." I raised my hand so that I could get her attention. "Would you mind if I went and used the bathroom?" I asked in anticipation for her answer.

"Yes, I really would mind RJ." Ms. Howard shook her head as she responded to me in a coy voice. "If you're asking me if you could go to the restroom, then sure."

Ms. Howard always tries to make things difficult for me and I don't understand it. I think she likes me. Well, maybe not. I walked out of the class room with my eyes half opened, still half sleep. I rushed to the bathroom, hoping that it would give me some type of energy to wake up. Aside from that, Aunt Jackie usually told me to call her in the mornings while I was in school so that she could check on me. Today was different from the other times because I didn't have the energy to call Aunt Jackie; I texted her instead. She wasn't really skilled at responding back to text messages because she said that it was confusing, but I didn't care and did not cut her any slack. After texting Aunt Jackie, she hesitated to respond, so I went back to study hall, still feeling a little sleepy.

The school day seemed so long and the sad thing about it was that it was only the beginning of the day. Once I walked back into the class room, I went back to my seat, opened up a random book as if I was about to read, then put my head down and went to sleep.

RJ, son I need you... You are the only thing that I have left... You are my future and my life... Please don't walk away from me... Please don't walk away from me RJ.

I suddenly woke up out of my sleep, only to hear the end of the first period's bell ringing. Waking up in fear, I rushed out of the door to move to my next class. I could already tell that this day was going to be one of the worst days of my life because my past was starting to haunt me. As I thought about my dream, I started feeling uneasy a little because it was so random. I was in the center of a baseball stadium somewhere and I could see the motion of the crowd cheering, but I couldn't hear any sound coming from their mouths. The only thing that I could hear was a voice telling me not to leave. While trying to pursue finding the distinct voice from the crowd, I noticed my brother Brandon sitting in his chair. As I rushed over to him to see what was wrong with him, he just kept repeating those words: '*RJ, son I need you... You are the only thing that I have left... You are my hope and my life... Please don't walk away from me... Please don't walk away from me, RJ*'. It was like my dad spoke through him, as if he was being controlled by my dad.

"RJ, what's wrong man?" Tim asked as my teacher, Mr. Ellis explained the objectives for the day.

Tim was one of my good friends that Aunt Jackie actually trusted me to hang out with. We entered high school together and have been very cool friends since then.

"Nothing Tim, I just had a crazy dream about my brother last class." I dazed out of the window across the room.

"So I'm guessing that you two conversation is more important than the one I'm having with the class?" Mr. Ellis called me and Tim out. I wanted to say yeah, but instead I just shook my head no and Mr. Ellis continued teaching the class; glancing back at me and Tim periodically.

"We'll talk later RJ." Tim whispered over to me as Mr. Ellis continued teaching the class. At that very moment, I felt like pouring out my entire dream to Tim and was starting to get impatient with the day already.

The hours started going by and school was finally almost over. Just as I raised my hand to go take another bathroom break, the bell rung. Mr. Harvard, my anatomy teacher seemed to rush us out of the class, as if he had a dinner date later on tonight or something. I didn't care though because I was ready to go and meet up with my family anyway. Although I had a long and boring school day, today was special to me because it was my brother, Brandon's birthday.

It was now 5:00 pm and Mr. Marvin allowed me to use the family car. I think that he and Aunt Jackie were in the process of buying me a car because I seen a lot of car advertisement papers around the house.

"I'll be back auntie." I yelled up the stairs to Aunt Jackie as Mr. Marvin tossed the keys to me from the kitchen.

"Ok, don't forget to call me boy!" I could hear Aunt Jackie yelling down the stairs.

I rushed outside, jumping in the car before they changed their minds about me using it. Pulling out of the neighborhood, I excitedly put T Soul's album, *Love and Music* into the CD player. I made plans to visit my mom's grave site today since I hadn't been in a long time.

Two lousy minutes went by when my cell phone instantly started ringing. My screen was messed up so I couldn't see who was calling me.

"Hello?" I turned the music down so that I could hear myself talking.

"RJ, didn't I tell you to call me when you got in the car boy!" Aunt Jackie is always cautious every time I leave out by myself.

"Auntie, you didn't give me enough time to call you!" I had to make sure I didn't respond too crazy or else Aunt Jackie would punch my teeth out my mouth when I got back home.

"I'm only picking Tim up so that he can go with me to visit my mom's grave site, then we were both heading back to the house."

I was nervous as to what Aunt Jackie's response was going to be because I forgot to tell her that I was going to pick Tim up and bring him over.

"Alright, well just call me once you leave the site." I was shocked to hear Aunt Jackie respond like that. I expected her to be upset that I didn't tell her about Tim coming over later.

"Iight auntie." I hung up the phone and turned the music back up. My dream from earlier came back to mind and it wouldn't leave me this time. "Man, I wish I knew where Brandon was." I said out loud as I continued thinking about that crazy dream from earlier.

A couple of minutes after I picked Tim up, we were on our way to the grave site to visit my mom. Tim was cool enough to buy some flowers so that I could put them on the grave stone. As we pulled up into Crestview grave site, my stomach started to drop. I was a little nervous about coming to visit my mom without having Aunt Jackie with me. Auntie always seemed to soothe me during these times because I would always seem to go off into a fit. We parked the car on the road path in the grave yard and got out. Tim didn't want to walk up to the site with me because he told me that it gave him nightmares.

Walking up to the site slowly and starting to shake, I began humming *His eye is on the sparrow*. My mom's stone was big as day, "Sylvia Jones, my mommy," was all I could say as I looked at the writings on the tombstone.

Tears began to fill my eyes and my eyelids released tear drops every time I blinked. As I reflected on the sweet and short memories I had of my mom, it brought more tears and sadness my way. I could tell that Tim was feeling a little sympathetic because he got out of the car. He walked up behind me while patting my back. He didn't bother me, but just remained silent as I had my time with my mom.

"Mommy, things aren't the same anymore." I began talking to her. "Everything seems weird now and it's like I'm lost in the sauce and left out of things I should probably know. Aunt Jackie is raising me up right, just as you would have done and Brandon is no where to be found and I really miss him." I began to cry even more. "Daddy is somewhere doing his own thing and honestly I don't like what I am hearing about what he did to Brandon. I need your support right now to make everything better again." I paused.

Tim was just as emotional as I was because he started wiping his eyes. It was like he knew exactly how I felt and he showed it as his emotions exposed him.

"Mommy I apologize, and this is my best friend Tim. He goes to school with me, very cool person." I looked at Tim as he smiled. Tim began to open up to my mom and kept telling her that he was going to look out for me and not to worry. I tell you, Tim was my right hand and I knew that I could depend on him for anything.

Within fifteen minutes of our time at the grave site, the night lights started to come on. The entire time that we were there, we were laughing and thinking about the childhood memories that I had with my mom, my dad and Brandon. As I glanced down to put the flowers on the ground, I noticed a folded up note next to the stone. I looked up at Tim to see if he had noticed it, but it was obvious we both were laughing too much to even see it. I opened up the note and as I unfolded the paper, I seen Aunt Jackie's name with a slash, then my name. I guess the note was for whoever got to it first. I stood straight up and unfolded the paper as I read it aloud.

'To Whom It May Concern, it is obvious that your here at the grave site because now your reading this letter. I don't want any problems or drama, but I do want to make you aware that I'm looking for my son.'

I automatically knew that it was my dad who wrote this note as fear made its way into the grave field. Tim and I ran back to the car and locked all of the doors while pulling off. I couldn't think and my heart was beating so fast. Tim kept asking me what was going on and what did the letter mean, but I was too afraid to explain everything. We pulled up to a red light and Tim got louder, demanding that I tell him what was going on once he noticed me shaking uncontrollably. My hands were sweating and my head was starting to hurt.

"Tim, I'll tell you everything later man, just leave me alone right now!" I yelled back to Tim as he got hype all over again.

"RJ, what are you afraid of?" I heard a voice coming from the back seat. I looked to the back and to my surprise it was my dad reaching up to the front saying, "Daddy, got you now!"

"RJ, RJ wake up man!" Tim yelled as I slowly opened my eyes, noticing that I was on the ground next to my mom's grave. I guess I blacked out once I read the note I found on the ground. "Let's get you home man." Tim helped me up from the ground and guided me back to the car. Tim took the initiative to me drive back to the house because he knew that I was out of it. While riding in the car, I kept looking back; thinking that someone would be there, when in reality, no one was. The letter didn't have a date on it, but the paper looked freshly crisp. I didn't have to say a word to Tim because he already figured some things out himself. I sat in the passenger seat of the car and began to reflect back on how I grew up to become afraid of my dad's presence. When I was younger, it was my dad who would bail me out of things and he always was a protector, not letting anyone get to me or Brandon. I started crying heavily as more and more thoughts popped up in my mind.

Tim couldn't even focus on the road because he was too concerned about what was going on in my head. Tim was also spiritually grounded and knew how to handle problems such as these.

"I speak in the authority of the Holy Ghost, lose yourself Satan from the mind of my friend RJ!" Tim exclaimed as I twisted and turned in my seat.

Tim was serious and I could tell that he meant business. During the time of his prayer, he placed his hand on my stomach and continued to murmur a silent prayer while driving. As Tim continued praying, I began to ease up as things started to transition back to normal. I couldn't figure out exactly what it was that was going on with me and I was starting to get scared all over again; like in my younger years. Tim placed his hand back onto the steering wheel and we drove in silence all the way to my house. All that I could think about was Brandon and the dream that I had with us at the baseball field.

"Happy birthday to you Brandon", I said while choking up on my words from the tears that I was crying. As we continued driving in silence, I turned up the radio back to T Soul's song, *Love and Music*.

Chapter Five

The sun made its way into my room, exposing light to my face as I woke up from my last night's sleep. I had to get dressed and ready for school, but I didn't feel like going because it was too much going on. I knew that I couldn't talk to anybody about what was going on with me and my family, so I had to just keep quiet. As I got out of the bed, I walked to the bathroom to get in the shower before getting dressed for school. Jamie was up because I could hear her crying from Aunt Jackie and Mr. Marvin's room. As I stood in the shower and let the showerhead pour onto my head, all that I could think about was what happened last night. I kept the note hidden because I didn't want Aunt Jackie to panic. She easily panicked if things went wrong, so I tried not to show signs or do anything to symbolize that something was bothering me. It's been a minute since I've heard Aunt Jackie's song and that was a good thing because it indicated that she was stress free.

While stepping out of the shower, I heard Mr. Marvin calling my name as he knocked on the bathroom door.

"RJ, come to my room when you get out, I got something for you man", Mr. Marvin yelled as if he was competing over noise.

I dried off and put on some fresh pair of underwear and my ball shorts, then brushed my teeth and went to the room to see what he wanted. Aunt Jackie was feeding Jamie before she got dressed for work while Mr. Marvin was ironing his clothes.

"Wassup Unc?" I was so nervous.

"Man, I didn't get a chance to talk to you yesterday because time didn't permit for us to talk, but I wanted to ask you if you were alright",

Mr. Marvin glanced at me before pouring more water into the iron for an increased steam effect.

"Oh, yeah I'm good", I was lying. "It's just that after Tim and I left the site, I instantly grew tired and wanted sleep. It was a while since I went to visit my mom, so I guess my emotions finally released", this lie was becoming comfortable and I just added more details to support it.

"Ok, I understand RJ", Mr. Marvin gave me one final look while Aunt Jackie remained quiet. "You know I'll always avail myself to you so that we could talk, whether it's about girls, or ministry, etc", I nodded Mr. Marvin off as he continued to talk.

"Ok cool, thanks Unc", I started walking back towards my room.

Mr. Marvin is a cool dude and over time, I established a real relationship with him because he was open minded and understanding. He always knew the right things to say when my Aunt Jackie wasn't in the mood and at times, I rarely had to explain the way I felt to Aunt Jackie because he was easily immune to my feelings and explained it better to her.

I got dressed kind of early today and was ready to start my day. I was glad because it was Friday and what made it even better was that we were having a shut in later on at our church tonight. It's interesting to me how we can change locations of residency, but stay in the same location for church. As I left out of the house, I walked up to the bus stop to wait for the bus, realizing that I was twenty minutes early. Instead of going back in the house like I normally would, I just waited those minutes out at the bus stop. I took the note from last night out of my pocket and reread every sentence on the paper. I think I want to study psychology when I go to college because I get so in depth with my thoughts. I started wondering how my dad knew the spot of my mom's burial and what made him place the note on her tomb stone the way that he did. My dad was smart and knew exactly what he was doing, I thought. However, I don't think that he wanted trouble just as he stated in the letter, so I began to feel a little cool about the situation; I just had a lot of questions.

The bus finally came and once I got on, I went all the way to the back of the bus to get a seat. As I headed to the back of the bus, I saw Tim and his female friend Ira sitting together, talking and laughing. Ira was interesting to me and I don't know why. I didn't exactly figure it out all the way, but I knew that she seemed very skeptical.

"Wassup RJ", Tim reached for a hand shake as Ira smiled and waved to me.

"Sup man", I said while meeting his hand half way before taking my seat.

Tim tried talking to me, but I just wasn't in the mood to have conversation. Just to show him that I felt like being antisocial, I pulled out my iPod and put my earphones in my ears. I guess it didn't bother Tim though because he directed his attention back to Ira.

As we approached the school, everyone instantly stood to their feet before the bus driver could open the door. Noise filled the bus as we all noticed the school principal coming to our bus, then that's when everyone rushed back to their seats. As Principal Wilson got on the bus, he grabbed the microphone in the front of the bus to get our attention.

"Good morning students, as you all may know, we have multiple drills that we do on the bus just in case of an emergency, so instead of exiting from the front of the bus you will be exiting from the back of the bus." Principal Wilson was calm.

I hated these type of drills because we had to jump off of the back of the bus and I didn't see the point of it Tim tried getting my attention to wait for him once I got off the bus, but I ignored him as if I didn't hear him. After jumping off that ratchet colored yellow school bus, I walked into the school building, heading to study hall with Ms. Howard. She was enthused today and overly dramatic and I could tell that today was going to run smoothly for us. My phone started vibrating heavily and I rushed to the bathroom once Ms. Howard called the role.

"Hey auntie." I whispered. I was trying not to be too loud

on my phone in the bathroom because phones weren't allowed in school.

"RJ, please remember that tonight is shut in at the church, so when you come home make sure you eat and do your homework", Aunt Jackie was telling me as if I didn't know already.

"Alright auntie", I hung up the phone so that I could go back into class.

The first bell was about to ring and I could tell by the emptiness of the halls. Once I sat in my seat, I pulled out my next class's notebook. I never did my homework at home because I took full advantage of study hall and used this time to do my homework. The intercom came on, demanding that everyone stood to pledge to the flag. "I pledge allegiance to the flag of the United States of America..." While everyone was pledging to the flag, I began reciting the covenant creed from my church. Call me deep if you want, but I knew that every time I recited the covenant creed, things were better for me. Everyone sat back in their seats and did their work, as Principal Wilson read over the school announcements. My phone vibrated again, but I tried to ignore it because it was quiet in the classroom and I didn't want to draw attention to myself.

"Have a great day, students."

Just as the announcements were done, the classroom resumed to their daily activities. Ms. Howard was touchable and sociable today, walking around assisting anyone who needed her help.

My phone started vibrating again and this time, it was back to back after I ignored it for the second time. I raised my hand to go to the bathroom, but Ms. Howard tried to give me a hard time.

"Why is it that every class, you must go to the bathroom?" Ms. Howard slowly, but surely started returning to her old ways.

"Ms. Howard I have to use the bathroom, I have no other reason." I tried to convince her so that I could tend to my phone.

"Alright, you lucky it's Friday because otherwise, I would make you wait!" Ms. Howard had a smirk on her face as I stood to my feet to walk out of the room. Then she continued, "Then you always seem to go at the same time everyday."

I just ignored her and walked out. I always wanted to get Aunt Jackie to punch Ms. Howard in the face, but I knew that it wasn't the Christian thing to do. My phone vibrated again for a third time and this time I was able to answer it without any hesitation. Figuring that it was Aunt Jackie who was calling me, I quickly answered. "Hey auntie, wassup", I said while looking into the mirror.

"This aint ya auntie nigga, this ya Cousin Ray!" My jaw dropped and my heart began racing.

"Oh, was sup cuz?" I chuckled in fear.

"How did you get my number?"

Ray came from the other end of the earth and I always knew that something was up when he started coming around, good or bad.

"Man ya homeboy, ya auntie's nigga gave it to me once I told him who I was." Ray talked so disrespectful and it annoyed me that he was calling.

"Ok so wassup?" I tried rushing Ray off the phone.

"Man nothing, I was just checking on you to make sure things were cool between you and ya pops", Ray started bringing up my dad again.

"Ray, it's been years since I've talked to my dad and you know that."

I was confused where all of this was coming from as fear built up even more. I knew that I would soon have to tell Aunt Jackie something because it was starting to overwhelm me.

"Nah man, I'm only messing with you." Ray started laughing as if things were a joke. "I called to see if you wanted to go with me to meet some of ya family on ya dad side this weekend at the family gathering that Aunt Sally throw's every year." Ray started going in full detail.

"Ray, no I'm good." I didn't hesitate one time. "I have a lot going on this weekend, including church so I'll be tied up." I lied again.

"Aight, its cool family." Ray seemed understanding. "I'll just tell everybody that you said wassup."

I didn't care about that side of the family because they didn't really do anything for me and I barely even knew who they were.

"Ok, thanks Ray." I hung up the phone before I got caught.

"Oh yeah Ray, don't give my number out to anybody yo." I was so serious.

"Man, I got you." Ray started laughing as if he was trying to play me.

As I hung up the phone to put it in my pocket, I still was confused about some things. While attempting to exit the bathroom, a taller and more structured figure entered. I was stopped at the door of the bathroom by Principal Wilson.

"Hey, RJ is everything alright bud?" Principal Wilson smiled at me very weirdly.

"Yeah, everything is cool Mr. Wilson." I said as I rushed back to my classroom.

"It must be payday." I said to myself as I opened the classroom door to join the rest of the class.

Chapter Six

March 8, 2008

An entire month had passed by as senior year of high school came to a close. Aunt Jackie always told me that this would be the year everything happened quickly. Because I didn't really value time while being a senior in high school, I felt like I didn't prioritize as much as I could have. One thing that I can say I'm proud of myself for is the effort to push forward in the beginning of the school year. I applied for major colleges like Virginia State University, Florida State University and Louisiana State University. However, as the school year passed along, I started to second guess my selections and wanted to stay a little closer to home. There was only a month left of school and my class trip to Italy was in three weeks. Although I knew that Aunt Jackie didn't have the money to pay for me to go, I knew that it wouldn't be a problem for Mr. Marvin to.

It was early Saturday morning and me and baby Jamie was watching Dora the Explorer on the nickelodeon channel. Although she really couldn't comprehend everything that was happening on the show, she was well alert. *"Dora Dora Dora the explorer..."* I sung to Jamie while she just watched me sing. Mr. Marvin was out at a deacon's meeting at church and Aunt Jackie was still upstairs sleep. Because I had major support from Aunt Jackie and Mr. Marvin, I tried not to think too much about the negative things that were happening all around me.

I popped open Jaime's bottle top to put in her mouth, at the same time I reached for my phone to call Tim.

"Hello." Tim said with a raspy voice.

"Yo Tim, wake up punk!" I was very energetic this morning, forgetting that it was still early.

Tim went out last night with his new girlfriend, Ira so I wanted to be nosey and see what happened on their date. At first, he didn't say too much about their festivities, but then he started to share more and more and open up as our conversation progressed. I started laughing when Tim said that Ira had milk dud nipples, but suddenly stopped once I heard footsteps coming down the stairs. Aunt Jackie let out one big disgusting yawn as she reached the bottom step. I could already tell last night that she was going to be exhausted because Jamie would not go to sleep.

"Good morning nephew." Aunt Jackie said as she walked towards the kitchen to start breakfast.

This was the first time in a long time that Aunt Jackie got up on a Saturday morning to cook breakfast and it kinda felt like old times again.

"Good morning auntie." I continued talking to Tim on the phone. "So like how do you really feel about her yo?" I asked hoping that he wouldn't respond too quickly.

"In all honesty RJ, I think I love her." I could hear Tim taking a deep breath after those words came out. I already knew that Tim was moving entirely too fast, but the type of person he is, he was a hardhead.

"Man, I think that you need to slow down Tim." I said cutting off his exhale. "You are too focused with your future and God to allow intruders to come into your life and distract you." I can be a little knowledgeable too guys; Ha! He wasn't trying to hear that though because he was too wrapped up in Ira's so called love. I knew that I had to be the one to rain on his parade though because nobody else actually would.

(Don't get me wrong folks, I'm not the jealous type of person, I am just protective of my friends and who they fall for; especially because girls are tricky. My Aunt always told me that wolves came in sheep's clothing, so I live by that every day. I really didn't know Ira well anyway, except for the times that she always smiled when I seen her. It wasn't one of those innocent smiles either, it was more of a sneaky one.)

"RJ I'll be the judge man." Tim laughed it off, trying to move to another trending topic. I could tell deep inside that Tim felt some type of way based off of what I was saying.

"RJ come here!" Aunt Jackie yelled from the kitchen. I told Tim that I would call him later, then hung up the phone and walked towards the kitchen with Jamie in my arms.

"Yes auntie." I was hoping that she wouldn't ask me to help her.

"Come and help me scramble these eggs." Aunt Jackie said while stirring the pancake batter.

I knew she would ask me to help her, dag. I put Jamie in her high chair and went to the refrigerator to take out some eggs.

"Now I know you have a lot going on nephew, being as though you're a senior, but I want you to be careful." Here she goes with the random conversations. I just listened to what it was she was saying because I didn't want to come off being disrespectful.

"In this next phase of your life, you will be challenged with real life stuff that will require your undivided attention. Now I'm telling you, you have to pay attention to the little details in life because they will be the ones that matter the most and I don't want you to get caught up in the traps of the enemy."

Aunt Jackie sure did know how to pull out the deep stamp. She went on and on about friendships and how I should always be aware of the people that fraud. "Watch out for those snakes baby." Aunt Jackie continued while pouring the stirred batter into the frying pan.

A whole hour later, we were on the couch full and nodding off to sleep. I'm telling you, after a good meal like that, you probably would be nodding off too. Aunt Jackie looked so peaceful over there lying on the couch as Jamie laid across her chest. I laid across the love seat trying so hard not to go to sleep, but that was an epic failure. I usually am up once I wake up the first time, but this time I guess was different. I turned on my IPod and put in my ear phones as I let the music take me away. I was temporarily stress free and feeling kind of good because I was at a good place in my life. I knew that this feeling wouldn't last for long though because things were going too smooth.

Minutes later, I heard my phone vibrating and I looked

down to see the broken screen display a notification, indicating I had a text message. Now everyone that has my number knew my screen was broke so I don't know what caused somebody to text my phone. Soon after my phone vibrated with a text notification, it vibrated again, notifying that someone was calling. I picked up the phone and to my surprise it was my big brother, Brandon.

"Hello... RJ are you there bro?" I was so excited to hear Brandon's voice, I felt like I was about to pass out.

"Yes, Brandon where are you because I miss you and need to see you!" I was all smiles. I hopped off of the couch and ran to my room to put on some clothes.

"I'm actually in your neighborhood." Brandon was a little hesitant.

"Ray told me where I could find you, so I hope you're not mad."

At this point, I didn't care because I really needed to see my brother. It was so much that we needed to catch up on and I needed to ask him a lot of questions. I left Aunt Jackie sleep on the couch with Jamie on her chest.

"It's cool brother, so where do you want me to meet you?" I put on some ball shorts and a tee shirt.

"I'm walking up to your door now." Brandon said it as if he was ready to walk right through the door.

"Alright, I'll be down in ten seconds." I hung up the phone. I looked at the picture of me and Brandon when we were little kids that stood on my dresser and smiled. Shutting my drawer full of clothes, I rushed back down the stairs, even skipping some.

As I got to the last step, I seen that Aunt Jackie and the baby were still sleep with the TV left on. I took a deep breath while smiling with a fast heart beat before opening the door. I opened the door and standing on the other side of the screen door was Brandon with a sad face, holding my dad's hand. My heart flew out my stomach as sweat ran from my forehead, hitting my eye ball.

"Why are you avoiding us RJ?" My dad was extremely angry and I could tell he wanted revenge. In his other hand was a briefcase with an illuminati symbol on it. "We came to pick you up RJ." My dad began yelling as he attempted to turn the knob.

"Dad, I'm not going anywhere!" I yelled back in response while tears poured out my eyes.

"RJ come on boy... You have us waiting out here!" My dad

screamed even louder while still trying to open the door. I looked to see Brandon crying out that he missed me in the midst of the commotion.

"RJ... RJ...RJAAAAY!" My dad yelled with a shallow voice, but then the tone got lighter as the echo continued fading away..

"RJ, wake up boy! What the hell are you screaming for?" Aunt Jackie was standing over top of me as she pulled the ear phones from my ears. I couldn't respond because Aunt Jackie was already on a hundred. She seemed very mad and didn't bother to move until I was fully up and alert.

"It was just a dream", I said to her as Jamie continued screaming from the top of her lungs.

"Hell, you scared me and the baby, boy!" Aunt Jackie put a bottle filled with apple juice in Jaime's mouth.

Everything began to settle as we heard the sound of keys rattling on the other side of the door. Mr. Marvin came in the house with Dunkin Doughnuts, which was my favorite. He went over to Aunt Jackie and kissed her on the cheek, then kissed Jamie on her forehead.

"Wassup nephew?" Mr. Marvin asked while putting the box of doughnuts on the center table in the family room.

"Nothing much." I responded, being scared that Aunt Jackie would tell him what just happened moments ago.

While reaching for a doughnut, I could see Aunt Jackie staring at me in my peripheral. "Boy you are truly a dreamer with a brain full of imaginations because that's my first time ever hearing you talk in your sleep." Aunt Jackie used her sense of humor to get the tension out the room. We all started laughing while eating doughnuts.

"Babe, I thought ya'll were going to be dressed." Mr. Marvin whined to Aunt Jackie.

"I just have to put on my clothes." Aunt Jackie smiled while forcing her index finger into his forehead.

"RJ go get dressed because we'll be heading out in a second." I went upstairs to get dressed without asking any questions.

Ten minutes had passed, just as I lotioned my arms before putting on my bracelet. Being a little curious, I pulled the note out that Tim and I found at the grave site from under my pillow. I read every sentence over, glancing up at me and Aunt Jackie's name on the envelope.

"You ready nephew?" Aunt Jackie surprisingly stood at my bed room door.

"Yes, I'll be down in a minute auntie."

I hope she didn't notice the paper I was holding in my hands because she catches on to stuff like that. She went down the stairs singing one of her favorite hymns. When I knew that the coast was clear, I instantly put the note back under my pillow and rushed down stairs after shutting my door.

We jumped in the car and pulled out the drive way. I didn't know where we were going, but I was ready to leave the house because that seems to be the only place I'm allowed to go. I needed to clear my mind because nightmares were starting to birth from my brain and I didn't know what was going to happen next.

I looked out of the window as we approached the highway, thinking about Brandon and where he might be. Twenty minutes later, we pulled into the parking lot of Dave and Busters, near the zoo Aunt Jackie used to take me when I was a kid. A smile formed on my face and excitement grew as I watched the Dave and Buster's sign rotating. I never been to Dave and Busters before and I knew that I was about to experience the best time of my life. We walked up to the entrance of Dave and Busters. As we stepped into the building, Mr. Marvin tried to get an employee's attention.

"May you escort us to the room reserved for Hall please?" Mr. Marvin was trying to sound professional. I didn't know what was going on and was trying to figure out why we were here as we followed the employee, but it wasn't enough time for me to do so. Aunt Jackie kept looking at me and smiling, causing me to get mixed signals and emotions. We stopped at the closed door ahead of us and I seen Mr. Marvin open the door, signaling me to walk inside.

"SURPRISE!!!" a crowd of family, friends, church saints and even teacher's yelled out while screaming at me.

"Happy Birthday RJ!" Aunt Jackie and Mr. Marvin said while giving me a hug. It was then that I knew something was wrong with me because it slipped my mind that my own birthday was tomorrow. I don't know how in the world I forgot that my birthday would soon be approaching. Was I that bothered that I didn't even remember? Everybody showed up at my party and I felt a little special. I stood looking in the crowd seeing Tim with Ira, Cousin Veronica with Asia and Jay, Aunt Jackie's God kids, Kailyn, Eric and Patrick, and even Lil Rodney. He blended in with all the rest of them, laughing with the other guest and what not. This was my time to enjoy myself with the people who cared most about me.

"Well go ahead and look at your cake RJ." Mr. Marvin was excited and smiled while directing me to the table.

"I wish my brother was here to help me celebrate." I said out loud as we walked toward the cake. I noticed Mr. Marvin facial expression change.

"Don't worry nephew, I'll make sure you see him soon."

Mr. Marvin seemed very confident about it. I didn't know how he was going to make it happen, but I had just enough faith in him that my dreams and prayers would come true.

Chapter Seven

March 9, 2008

My birthday was great and I was hype about all of the gifts I received from people. It barely hit me that I was eighteen years old because everything almost seemed the same. Same issues, same emotions and most of all, I still felt like the same person. In all of my years of living, I always had to prove myself to people because my presence alone wasn't enough and didn't leave space for people's faith in me. In grade school, I would always try to fit in by doing things that I seen others do and say the very things that they would say. My aunt would always tell me to be a leader and not a follower so I had to transition from walking with many to none at all. Brandon was all I had growing up and then when he left, I felt like I was by myself. In middle school many people started to become attracted to my personality as if they seen something in me all of a sudden. I mean, yeah I was a church boy and isolated myself from harm's way, but I still seemed to keep their interest. I was very touchable and tried my best to keep it real with them, but was also careful with what I said around certain individuals and how I said it. One thing that I was very knowledgeable of was who to entertain and who to flee from. The flip side to all of that was that no matter what I did that was right, I still felt miserable. I try to make my happiness last a life time, but evil always seems to haunt me. It's like nothing can ever be good around me because everything is always bad. I truly believed that I was cursed by somebody and I don't know who; I promise I'm not crazy though.

(Now, I'm not trying to give you a sob story or tell you about myself so that you could be on my side, but I just wanted to make a point that you can't judge a book by its cover. No matter how confident someone may be in thinking that they have you figured out, reality is that no one knows another person unless they have completely walked in their shoes.)

I was standing in the front yard of Cousin Veronica's house. Aunt Jackie had to catch up on the latest gossip or catch cousin Veronica up I guess because she was too anxious to get over here. It was one of those days where nothing was really happening in the neighborhood and everything around was just there. I felt like I was in a western movie, only to realize that I was in the ghetto. As I sat on the steps, I scoped a few junkies, drug dealers and little kids fighting over a car toy; that was really it.

"RJ, come here for a second." Cousin Veronica's son, Jay said to me.

It was quite interesting that he was eager to hold conversation with me because I just knew he hated my guts. We went to his room and all that he did was surf the internet. Aunt Jackie was in the living room getting her hair done by Cousin Veronica while they continued gossiping.

"What's this?" I asked as I focused more on the screen as Jay scrolled down.

"It's a website that allows you to connect with other teens so that you can challenge each other in different games." Jay was focused on the screen, not giving me eye contact.

One thing about Jay is that he's definitely a computer freak. He has an interest in video games and other discoveries on the internet and is passionate about it. However, surfing the web is the least of my worries because I am too worried about my personal life. What made it worst was that I put a lot of unnecessary stuff on myself, realizing that some things are not that serious to worry about. I couldn't enjoy my last bit of teenage years because it felt like I had so many problems of my own that prevented me from embracing my youth.

"That's cool." I said as Jay entered into a new game.

"So tell me RJ, what's going on with you?"

Jay was trying to be nice. Because I was just starting to experience a new level of maturity with Jay, I was a little skeptical on how to embrace it or him.

"What you mean Jay?" I really wanted to avoid his

questions.

"Let's be mature about this RJ, you know what I mean. It's like your falling off, for real." Jay started shaking his head.

I didn't know how to take that last statement he made and I was starting to get mad.

"I'm not falling off and for the record, as long as you know who you are and what you about, then that's all you need to know!" I had to let it out. "You just like ya mom; Stop wanting to know the business of others because honestly speaking, you can't do anything for me."

My body temperature started getting hot as I expressed myself more and more. The shakes took over as anger formed into my eyes, causing me to put my wall up. Jay was speechless and tried to brush off what I was saying to him, but I knew he heard what I was saying. After my remarks to him, I went to the bathroom to rush water on my face. I shut the door behind me and said a quick prayer just to calm me down.

"For thine is the kingdom and the power and the glory forever amen." I prayed while turning the water knob on.

I looked into the mirror and my face looked a little distorted. My eyes were red and I could literally feel anger growing more and more in my stomach. I bust the bathroom door open and walked back into Jay's room. He was still surfing the net when I got to his door. Everything got crazy from there because I blacked out once I walked up to his face. Moments later, Cousin Veronica and Aunt Jackie rushed up the stairs. Of course Cousin Veronica made it up the stairs first because I heard her yelling once she got to the top of the stairs.

"Jackie, these bastards up here fighting!" Cousin Veronica said as she ran into the room, pulling me off of Jay. Aunt Jackie finally got to the top of the stairs and went bananas.

"Get off of me!" I yelled as Cousin Veronica held me down.

I could tell that Jay was scared because once she parted us; he sat on his bed in silence.

"What in the hell is going on?" Aunt Jackie asked.

"I want him out of my business! He needs to worry about his own self!" I couldn't stop screaming.

I noticed that I was releasing childhood anger I had towards him that he probably never imagined me having.

"No... Body knows the trouble I see, nobody knows but me!!" Aunt

Jackie sang repeatedly while looking worried. I could tell that something was about to happen because she only would sing that if she noticed a change, whether it be in an environment or a person. Tears started to fall onto my face and I stormed out of the room. I could hear Cousin Veronica and Aunt Jackie asking Jay what happened and what sparked my fire, but he couldn't seem to give an answer because he was just as confused as they were. It's funny how people could torture and treat you bad over the years, and then once you explode, it's a sudden surprise like they didn't see it coming.

"Let's go, now!" Aunt Jackie said as she pulled me down the stairs.

I knew that she was in total shock with me because I wasn't the type of person to explode the way I did. We got in the car and pulled off from their block.

"Now, what were ya'll doing upstairs RJ?" Aunt Jackie asked while putting on music. She didn't wait for me to respond. "I'm so glad that you knocked some sense into that boy because he was really asking for it!" Aunt Jackie's attitude instantly shifted once we pulled off and drove home.

Aunt Jackie was my favorite, not because she defended me all the time, but because she understood me. It would be other times where I didn't have to say a word and she could just pick up on the way I was feeling. I started to ask her why she yoked me up like that, but I guess it was a part of the show. I don't know, but I knew that she just had better apologized when she did because she was going to get knocked out next; Nah, I'm kidding. Things got back to normal as we got closer and closer to the house. Cousin Veronica called Aunt Jackie to see if everything was cool, then next thing I know, they were back gossiping again.

We finally pulled up in the drive way and from a distance, I could see Lil Rodney sitting on his steps. I opened my door to get out of the car and as I shut my door, I seen Ray coming from the inside of Lil Rodney's house. Before I noticed Ray coming out the house, me and Lil Rodney locked eyes, so I knew he seen Aunt Jackie pulling up. I just hoped that Ray didn't see me because I was trying to avoid him as much as I could. I was a little skeptical about Lil Rodney as well, but with Ray, it was a deeper feeling I had.

We got in the house and as we opened the door, I could smell the aroma of food. It smelled like peppers and onions and tomato sauce. I was almost sure Mr. Marvin was making spaghetti. In my peripheral, I could see Mr. Marvin with his chef apron on in the kitchen.

"Babe we home!" Aunt Jackie said as she kicked off her pumps and sat on the couch. Jamie was sleep in her vibrating chair.

"Welcome, welcome." Mr. Marvin said as he gave Aunt Jackie a kiss on the lips.

"Wassup RJ?" Mr. Marvin said jokingly as he walked back into the kitchen.

"Unc, the same ole same ole." I said as he laughed from the kitchen.

"I know what you mean boy." He walked over to give Aunt Jackie a taste of the spaghetti sauce from his cooking spoon.

Minutes later, the spaghetti was finished and we all sat at the dinner table to eat. My phone kept vibrating, but I ignored it because Aunt Jackie was watching to see if I would answer it during family time. Mr. Marvin tried creating conversation as we ate, just to make family time a little entertaining.

"Sooooo what's new folks?" Mr. Marvin asked smiling, while glancing at Aunt Jackie.

"Why are you looking over at me?" Aunt Jackie said while chuckling.

"Everything is cool over here, brotha." She said while trying to give him daps.

I loved being around my aunt and uncle because they had a banging relationship, well that's what I thought anyway. They were so cool with each other and wasn't the serious type of couple, but was rather fun.

"RJ, what's new my dude?" Mr. Marvin asked, I guess trying to sound like he's down with the get down.

"Nothing much Mr. Marv." I said while wrapping spaghetti noodles around my fork. "Everything is the same, nothing changed."

"Oh yeah?" Mr. Marvin asked as if he knew something that I wouldn't say. "Your cousin Ray came over a little before you guys came home, asking for you, is everything ok?" Mr. Marvin asked while eating his spaghetti.

"To my understanding, Aunt Jackie doesn't want me around him because he is trouble." I looked over at Aunt Jackie.

"That's right and he is not to come over here looking for

you again."

Aunt Jackie had put on a slight serious face. Mr. Marvin and I could tell by the look on her face that she was serious. I don't know why Mr. Marvin made mention of that while Aunt Jackie was around.

"Babe, next time he comes around, tell him that I want to speak with him." Aunt Jackie said as if she was going to curse Ray smooth out.

"Oh please, Jackie." Mr. Marvin said while dropping his fork on his plate. "That boy is no trouble; he just wants to be loved." Mr. Marvin seemed sincere about what he was saying. He was starting to scare me though because he felt the opposite of what the rest of the family felt.

"Marvin, please." Aunt Jackie said while taking a sip out of her cup. "That boy is trouble and that's that; point, blank, period. Stop trying to defend everybody, Deacon Marvin." Aunt Jackie continued while shaking her head. She tried to keep her face as serious as possible, but she couldn't hold back her smirk. We all began laughing making jokes about their titles in the church.

"If you say so, Missionary Jackie!" Mr. Marvin said as we all laughed, even harder.

Chapter Eight

March 12, 2008

    School was starting to get on my nerves because everything was starting to slow down it felt like. One thing about me is that I hate anticipation, so upcoming events started to kill me because I had to anticipate, rather than it just happening right away. It was 2:10 in the afternoon when school let out. Our class trip was in a week so I had to figure out a plan to get extra spending money so that I could get souvenirs in Italy. I guess Aunt Jackie and my Mr. Marvin put their funds together for my senior class trip because they kept mentioning how thankful I'd better be. I was on my way to the locker to put away my backpack when I was stopped by Tim's girl, Ira.

    "Hey boo!" Ira said to me smiling, while handing me a picture.

    The word "boo" had became a common and popular term used by everyone as a greeting relating to a significant other in a relationship outside of those who were deeply in love.

    "Wassup Ira? What's this?" I asked in curiosity as I viewed the picture she handed me in excitement of her and Tim. They must have gone to a picture studio to get pictures taken because the quality of the photo was good.

    "You like?" Ira asked while chuckling.

    I was starting to get mixed feelings about Ira at this point and it was starting to be a little confusing because I liked her. (Well, let me clear it up for you, not exactly like her in the way you're thinking, but she was a cool cat.) I started laughing uncomfortably. I could tell that she was a little clueless because of the length of my laugh.

    "What's funny?" She asked as if she missed something that

I seen in the picture.

"Oh, nothing." I said quickly so that she wouldn't get mad. "Ya'll really serious about this relationship I see." I said while opening my locker.

"I mean, why wouldn't we be?" She asked as if I was her worst enemy.

I didn't feel the need to respond, so I quickly shut my locker and smiled. Smiling was a way for me to transition into another conversation when things seemed awkward.

"Imma catch up with you later Ira." I said to her as she gave me a blank look. I think she wanted to keep the conversation going, but it wasn't going anywhere because she always got offended.

As I approached the bus, my phone vibrated. I didn't feel like checking to see who it was that was calling me. I sat down in my seat and looked out the window at the clouds.

'There is no place I would rather be than to be on this bus right now.' I thought to myself while pondering. I started feeling uneasy. I couldn't get my hands on what it was though. No longer did I want to face anything that the world had to offer because I felt like there was no point of it anymore. The bus ride seemed short because it felt like I was at the entrance of my town home's development within seconds. As I got off the bus, I started to feel my pockets in search of my keys while stepping onto the street ground. The only thing that I could feel in my pocket was my cell phone. As I pulled out the phone, I saw that it was a missed call from Aunt Jackie. I started to worry because I didn't know if she was calling me just to tell me that she would pick me up from school or if she had instructions for me when I got home. While trying to dial her number, my phone died and I really started to worry because missing one of her calls was like missing the school bus in the morning. I just knew I charged my phone last night because that's my normal routine every night before going to bed. As I looked out in a distance towards my house, I looked across the street towards Lil Rodney's house.

Today, the neighborhood was dead and eerie. There were a few people out, mainly the dope heads and little kids playing at the community park. I walked up to my house, hoping that someone would answer the door. Mr. Marvin usually was home round this time and would park his car in the garage, but I knew that Aunt Jackie wasn't home yet. I knew that she would soon be on her way though. Too much was running through my mind and it was starting to cause my bladder to fuel up with yellow, human liquid. "I have to pee!" I said out loud as I patiently waited for someone to answer the door. No one came to the door, so I had to think quick. I looked over to Lil Rodney's house again, noticing the door cracked open. "Nah." I thought to myself before allowing my mind to create a new thought about going over to Lil Rodney's. I couldn't afford to go over there because I probably wouldn't come out and I also knew that Aunt Jackie wouldn't approve. My bladder had reached its limit, so without hesitation, I ran over to Lil Rodney's house. At this point, I could care less what Aunt Jackie said. I could almost hear her voice in the back of my head. "Aunt Jackie, I'm sorry but ya boy gotta do what he gotta do!" I said to myself while laughing. I got to the steps of the door and knocked until someone came to the screen door.

"Aye yo, who dat?" I could hear a voice from inside yelling towards the front door. Before I could open my mouth to tell the unidentified voice who I was, they came to the screen door. To my surprise, it was Ray. "Oh, was sup cuz?" Ray said while opening the screen door to let me in.

Ray was a fraud and he seemed unbelievable, like fake. He was always nice to me and when Aunt Jackie would come around, he turned on the mega nice switch. I didn't know what that was about, but I knew that it was weird.

"Hey, can I come in and use the bathroom?" I asked while he opened the door as if he was forcing me to come in before I even asked.

"Yeah nigga, ca ca come in." Ray started stuttering.

I guess, every time he gets high, it causes him to be goofy and choke on his words. That's the only thing I could come up with to explain him stuttering. Ray and Lil Rodney smoked weed all day, every day and it was bad. I started to wonder how Lil Rodney's parents felt about it, but they never seemed to be around. Ray told Aunt Jackie once before that Lil Rodney's mom was in some sort of trouble with the law and always got arrested and his dad was constantly on the road, traveling back and forth to take care of his grandma who was in the nursing home. Lil Rodney had a lot of freedom and didn't know how to maintain it.

"Yo Ray, who dat cuz?" I could hear Lil Rodney yelling from the other room. The front room was cloudy and the smell of marijuana filled the air. I could see his silhouette coming through the fog. "Oh aight, wassup RJ?" Lil Rodney said while coming out the other room with a blunt in his hand.

I promise, it was like after they both smoked one entire blunt, they would roll another one. The air was thick and it was easy for someone to catch contact if they were in the house long enough. I captured those thoughts I was thinking in my mind and went to the bathroom. I walked in the bathroom and shut the door as fast as I could, pulling down my pants. (Isn't it funny how people really get the urge to pee when they finally get to the toilet?) As I began aiming, I closed my eyes and it was like I went to another planet that protected me from harm. I usually have weird fantasy illusions and that's fine because it exercises my way of thinking.

There was a bang on the bathroom door, causing my aim to miss the toilet water and hit the seat.

"Yeah!" I shouted to the door while pulling my pants up and grabbing toilet paper from the roll to wipe the seat.

"Yo, Aunt Jackie at the door!" Ray said as his voice started to fade out from the other end of the door. I knew that I would be in a world of trouble when our eyes locked because out of everybody I came in contact with, Aunt Jackie protected me from Lil Rodney and Ray the most. I opened the bathroom door slowly, thinking that Aunt Jackie would be standing in the hallway with a bat in her hand.

While walking through the hall, I could hear Aunt Jackie's voice loud and clear. "Is this all ya'll do all day?" I heard Aunt Jackie ask. "It's a mess in here and another thing, why is the air in here so thick?" Aunt Jackie went on and on, not leaving space for Ray or Lil Rodney to talk. I walked into the front room and seen Aunt Jackie standing at the front door as if she was mad at the world. "And Rodney, I'm very surprised with you because you told me that you were a leader." Aunt Jackie said while looking directly at Ray.

"Aunt Jackie, I am!" Lil Rodney said while smiling.

I knew that he was embarrassed, but he tried so hard not to show it. I kind of felt sorry for Ray though because he looked innocent and seemed out of it. I guess he just zoned Aunt Jackie out because the entire time she was talking, he just sat on the couch in silence.

"RJ come on, I don't even know why you were in here!" Aunt Jackie continued going off as I walked out of the house. "Now if the cops were to bust in that house, you would be going to jail with the rest of those bastards!" Aunt Jackie said as we walked across the street.

I could always tell when she was extremely upset about something because once she starts, it's no turning back. We got to the house and as I looked back, I could see Lil Rodney and Ray on the porch shaking their heads at Aunt Jackie. I started to say something to her so that she could look back and respond to them, but I ignored it and just walked inside the house.

As I walked in the house, it was like everything just stopped. There was so much negative energy in the room and it was starting to make me feel sick. I could literally see my heart beating through my shirt. Mr. Marvin was sitting on the couch with his feet on the table and his head back, facing the ceiling. Normally, he would be the one that initiated conversation every time I walked in the door from school, but this time Aunt Jackie played that role.

"What were you doing over there?" she asked in frustration. "I left my keys at home. So I ran home from the bus stop. I was knocking on the door to see if someone would answer." I started to slowly loose breath. "No one answered and I had to use the bathroom, so I walked across the street to Lil Rodney's house and asked if I could use his bathroom." I continued as I noticed Mr. Marvin slowly tilt down towards my direction. "I don't trust them and I better not see you over there again!" Aunt Jackie said while looking at Jamie.

Mr. Marvin got up and walked towards the kitchen. Aunt Jackie looked at me and her entire mood changed, I promise she's bipolar. I noticed her eyes watering as she went and picked up Jaime from her bouncer. I was completely confused. I didn't know why she started to cry. She didn't even sing her song that symbolized danger or fear. 'Mr. Marvin is leaving', I thought to myself as I noticed him come from the kitchen with a piece of paper in his hand.

"What's going on?" I asked as Aunt Jackie cried even more.

She placed Jamie in her play pin and sat on the couch, trying to get herself together. Mr. Marvin seemed bothered too because he had a sympathetic look on his face once he came back into the room. They both looked at me and I just knew that I was in trouble because I thought they found the letter I was hiding from them. I was always taught that whatever happens in private will come out and since I was hiding this letter from them, exposure had come. Mr. Marvin handed me the paper and as I reached for it, I seen that it was a newspaper article. The headline's story title read, *"Teen Dead And Family Missing"*

"What does this have to do with me?" I asked as they encouraged me to read more. I started to read the beginning of the story and could feel a knot forming in my throat. "My brother!" I yelled with devastation, as my heart dropped to my stomach.

I couldn't believe what I was reading because it didn't seem real to me. I threw the paper onto the floor and fell to my knees. "My brother is dead, who killed him?" Was all I could ask because at that moment, my mind couldn't think about anything else. Aunt Jackie and Mr. Marvin tried comforting me, but it wasn't working at all. "Where is my dad?" I asked while looking at Aunt Jackie. She was speechless and didn't respond, so I continued asking while getting louder and louder. I didn't want to live life anymore once I read this tragic story about my brother. I literally seen his name printed on the paper next to the word, murdered.

"Your dad killed him RJ!" Aunt Jackie responded in rage. "That bastard and his new family set up my nephew!" She said as if she was trying to convince herself that it happened that way.

I was speechless and couldn't think. Too many thoughts were running through my mind all at once. I wanted to be alone and run away from everyone and never come back. Tears continued to run down my face as my body started to get numb all over.

"My brother is dead!" I screamed from the top of my lungs.

I started feeling dizzy as I screamed louder and louder. I noticed that everything around me started to turn into motion without the noise. My body became lifeless as I felt myself hit the floor. I could see Aunt Jackie and Mr. Marvin talking, but no sound coming out of their mouths. I got up from the floor and started walking towards the steps, but before I knew it, I fell back down and blacked out.

Chapter Nine

"RJ...RJ...RJ how you feel baby", I could hear Aunt Jackie's voice, but I didn't have the energy to respond. I couldn't even open my eyes because my body shut down, still feeling numb. A childhood memory flashed through my mind like in a movie.

"I love you brother." Brandon said while getting up to give me a hug and a kiss on my cheek. We were upstairs waiting for direction for us to come back downstairs.

"Brandon, stop I'm not a baby." I said while laughing and wiping off my cheek.

"You're my baby brother and it's nothing you can do about it." Brandon gave me another kiss on the cheek. He walked out of the room and started smiling, trying to be sneaky and listen to what was going on downstairs.

"Where are you going Brandon?" I asked as I seen him sit on the top of the steps. I didn't want to get in trouble, so I shut our bedroom door and pulled out my coloring book.

The memory started to transition into a horrific one just like that. It's like everything that was good turned bad. Within minutes, I could hear footsteps coming up the stairs and as I looked towards the door, I seen my dad with Brandon in his arms. I jumped up from out of my dream and started panicking.

"What's wrong baby?" Aunt Jackie said while rubbing my hand. I noticed that I was in a hospital bed and had an I.V tube in my arm.

"What happened?" I asked as Aunt Jackie asked the same thing, but for another reason.

The room was still and the silence broke once a nurse came rushing to my side of the room.

"Is everything alright?" The nurse asked while breathing a little heavy.

"Yes, he's fine." Aunt Jackie responded while smiling and continuing to rub my hand. "He must have had a bad dream." Aunt Jackie said in her professional voice.

I was thinking in my head that she was a fraud because she did it too well. As soon as the nurse left, Aunt Jackie got up from the bed and shut the room door behind the nurse.

"Boy you gonna get us kicked out of here, screaming like that!" She laughed as she tried to brighten up the mood in the room. One thing I could say about Aunt Jackie is that she's excellent in transitioning something bad into good. She never liked a dull environment and always encouraged positive energy wherever it lacked. It was now 3:13 am and I was still trying to figure out why I was in this hospital. I hate hospitals with a passion. I hate everything about them. From the smell to the people and the different rooms and food, my affection for hospitals never existed. The hospital to me represents bad news because nothing good comes out of it, but death. I think I was even more mad because I knew that Aunt Jackie wouldn't allow me to go on the class trip after this.

"The nurse said that you have to drink plenty of liquids so that you can get better sweetheart." Aunt Jackie handed me the half-melted jello that was saved from the dinner served earlier.

"Auntie, I don't want that right now, can I just know what's going on", I really was confused and began staring into her eyes.

"Well RJ, I was just telling you what the nurse told me." Aunt Jackie wasn't following what I was asking her.

"I'm talking about my brother Brandon, I want to know what really happened to him."

I think she noticed the tone in my voice changing. I was

extremely frustrated because I just wanted to know in full detail what was happening around me. I also knew that Aunt Jackie didn't have all of the answers to every question, but at this point I wanted her to. Rage grew in my stomach every time Aunt Jackie choked up when explaining how she thought the situation went down. Plus, I could not stay focused for the life of me because she would get side tracked and start telling other stories within the story.

"Aunt Jackie, please, could you just cooperate with me and let me know what's going on?" I said while taking the hospital sheets off my legs. My body started getting hot. It felt like steam was being released from my ears and I could tell that she was slowly but surely catching on to my mood.

For the first time in my life, Aunt Jackie didn't bother to go off on me and punch me in my arm like she would usually do when I talked back. Heck, she probably didn't do anything because she knew she would get in trouble if she were to since I was in the hospital.

"Ok, ok, ok RJ." Aunt Jackie said.

I could tell that she was holding something from me because of the long breath she took.

"The case regarding your brother is under investigation." Aunt Jackie took a sip of the free ginger ale the nurse gave her. I started to think about everything all over again, but didn't feel the need to interrupt her. "I really can't tell you how, but I knew Brandon was sent to the state and shipped to a foster home. I guess your dad couldn't take care of him and I tried to get custody over him, but the way the laws are nowadays, it's hard. Apparently, I wasn't eligible to be considered his guardian, so it was nothing I could do." There was a sudden knock on the door.

"May I come in? It's Nurse Sonia." I could hear a soft and shallow voice speak as Nurse Sonia knocked on the door.

"Sure, come in." Aunt Jackie said while fixing the sheets on my bed.

The nurse must have thought we were sleeping because she tip toed all around the room, before taking my vitals. She then tried making conversation, but I began to get mad because Aunt Jackie and I were already having our own private conversation. I didn't want Aunt Jackie to get too side tracked by the little talk they were having because we had more to cover and I knew she was nowhere near done.

"It looks like everything is fine." Nurse Sonia said while writing in her pad. "You have a minor temperature, but it should be down in the morning when the doctor comes back in to see you." I was happy to hear that because it gave me enough hope that I could possibly be leaving in the morning to go home.

"Thank you nurse." Aunt Jackie said while rubbing my hand like she does when we have visitors.

"Don't forget to drink plenty of liquids to keep you hydrated." Nurse Sonia opened up the door to leave the room.

"And then there were two!" Aunt Jackie said, trying to be funny while fixing my pillows.

"Auntie, we have to continue where we left off because we were getting warmer and I know it's not gonna take much for things to get hot." I was really anxious to know about everything that Aunt Jackie already knew.

"We'll talk about it later nephew, now go to sleep. It's almost four thirty in the morning boy." Aunt Jackie gave me a kiss on the forehead like she used to do when I was younger.

I was pissed, but tried to make her promise to continue the conversation in the morning. She acted like she couldn't hear me as she listened to her iPod with her eyes closed. It made me feel dumb because it looked like I was talking to myself while she was sleep. I glanced up at my monitor screen and seen the lines moving up and down, up and down with numbers beside them that were for I don't know what.

I laid my head on my pillow and looked up at the ceiling in amazement. All I could think about was my brother being where my mommy was and how they left me here with Aunt Jackie. I considered it to be a punishment because with the over protection of Aunt Jackie, I never had the chance to do what I wanted or live the life of a regular kid. Aunt Jackie always told me that I would appreciate it once I got older and I always said that I hoped so; in my head though. I closed my eyes and went into another world. It was bright all around with a pond that I seen kids playing at. They had on all white with little wings in the back of them and they were unsupervised like how me and Brandon were at times we were in our neighborhood. I walked through this neighborhood a little more and seen white dogs with wings, giraffe's with wings and even monkey's with wings and a lot of people with smiles on their faces as if they had nothing to worry about. I was satisfied with this new world that I discovered and wanted to stay and never return back to my world.

The air was refreshing and unpolluted and the houses were mouth dropping. I tried to walk up to one of the houses, but I was stopped by a gate, a major one. I had never seen a gate so wide and long before. The gate started to branch up from the ground, separating me from the freedom I discovered. "Is this heaven?" I screamed out to the people that consistently smiled at me, but no one responded. Moments later, I found myself on the outside of the gate, gripping the bars with all that I had within me. I tried looking for Brandon and mommy while being on the other side of the gate, but it was so much distraction from the amazement that my eyes were witnessing. Out of nowhere, I could hear laughing and barking on the same side I was on and when I looked, it was black creatures running in slow motion towards me. They looked like dogs, but had faces like possums. Their tails were long like a leopard and they had droopy black skin like a human. These dogs started to run faster and faster, barking and laughing, like hyenas. They seemed mad at me and ran as if they wanted to destroy me and even tear me into pieces.

I started to run from the gate that kept me safe and sane, into the wilderness that I discovered to be a catastrophe. I was running for my life, but I didn't know where I was running to because there was nowhere for me to go. I looked back to the gates and everything started to get dimmer and dimmer as I got further away from them. All of a sudden, war was going on all around me, but I didn't get caught up in it. The dogs seemed to still be chasing me and as I got further away from the gates, the creatures got bigger and bigger; transforming into human-like beasts. They started to call my name like they knew me as they continued laughing. It was like they would continue to run, but knew not to get close to me because they were waiting for me to drop and fall on my own. I screamed out for help and black rain drops started to burst from the dark-reddish clouds. I was running to a place that I knew was hell and as I tried to turn around to go another route, everything lead into one direction. I was trapped by desolation and deprived into thinking that I was escaping, when in all actuality the creatures were sent to draw me back to the place I came from; like dogs that go in search for stray sheep.

While going deeper and deeper into this dark place, I could

see my neighborhood and my school and even my shattered looking church. I tried running there, but was cut off by a deep hole in the ground, separating me from my church. The people around me were not smiling, but laughing because I was trying so hard to get back to everything that I lost.

"Why are you tryna escape boy? This is home." A black gloomy looking angel said to me while continuing to laugh. All the people started to say my name together, while pointing and laughing at me. I was the center of attention and could feel my insides burning in disgust and pain. "RJ Hill... RJ Hill... RJ Hill", the people kept calling me as if they knew me personally as I hurdled up into a ball. I looked up into the black sky and seen a bright red light covering me, like a spotlight.

"RJ Hill." I heard a distinct voice say in a distance but I didn't even care to see who it was that was calling me. It was like time had paused and the dark fog cleared up because I didn't see anyone anymore.

"RJ, wake up the doctor will be here to see you." Aunt Jackie said as I started to open my eyes. "Oh my Lord, why are your eyes so red baby, you don't look the same." Aunt Jackie started singing her song as she wiped the sweat from my face.

"I'm alright auntie, please just give me some time." I didn't want Aunt Jackie to do anything out of the norm. It was like she had discerned a bad spirit in me that I didn't know was there. She picked up her phone and called Mr. Marvin.

"Baby where are you at?" She focused on my every move and stared me dead in my face. Aunt Jackie paused with hesitation and fear. "It's gotten personal now". She said as she pulled the holy oil out of her purse and took off the top.

Chapter Ten

March 22, 2008

It was 10:15 am and the doctor gave the approval for me to be released from the hospital today. Before I could leave, Aunt Jackie had to sign all of these papers, just so that I could get discharged. My mind was racing and I couldn't keep the dream off my mind. It was one of those deep dreams that confused me because so much was going on in it. I wanted to tell Aunt Jackie about the dream, but she probably would brush it off, being as though she thinks something's wrong with me anyway. As we got to the entrance of the hospital, Mr. Marvin was already waiting for us in the drive thru entrance. I took a picture of me on my phone, just to see if things changed with my face and once I looked, everything seemed ok. Aunt Jackie was still talking about it in the car though and was convinced that she seen Satan himself in me.

"Babe, look at his face!" Aunt Jackie yelled as she put on her seat belt. Mr. Marvin looked at me, trying to figure out exactly what Aunt Jackie was talking about, then turned back around as he started to drive off the hospital grounds.

"Everything seems fine babe, you trippin." He said while laughing at Aunt Jackie. Mr. Marvin told Aunt Jackie that she was seeing things and that she needed to get her life together.

I personally didn't like what she was saying about me and it started to scare me because I started to wonder how it felt to have a demon inside of you. Aside from that, I still wanted to know about my brother's murder. The things that we didn't get to cover last night frustrated me.

"Yes Jesus loves me, yes Jesus loves me, yes Jesus loves me for the bible tells me so." I started to sing songs to ease my mind from the fear. Mr. Marvin continued driving and I could see Aunt Jackie in the mirror glancing at me with a disturbing look on her face. I started to think, is it me or Aunt Jackie that's going crazy because she really seems too involved with her personal feelings at times. My phone vibrated and I didn't want to answer it because I didn't want anybody calling with sympathy or praying for me over the phone. I looked down at my phone, realizing that it was a missed call from an unknown caller. I waited a couple of seconds just to see if they would leave a voicemail and to my surprise, they did. Usually, I don't condone these type of things, but I felt like being risky so it was acceptable today.

'Please enter your password, followed by the pound key.' The tone calling lady said as I called to check my voicemail. 'You have one new message, today at 10:56 am.' My stomach started to fill with butterflies and my heart started to race.

"Hey RJ it's me, Tim." I was confused and started to wonder why Tim was calling me from an unknown number. "Man I think your right about Ira because she's starting to trip for no reason and I'm confused. I called you from Alex Gardener's phone because Ira decided to throw my phone from a 10 leveled building when we were site seeing. I'm going to call you later when I get some free time on my hands, peace."

I saved the message in my phone and hung up, thinking how right I was about Ira. I don't mean any harm, but usually when I feel a certain way about a person, I'm usually right. Ira seemed very sneaky and she wanted attention at all times when she felt like nobody was giving her any. I could see her now in Italy, trying to boss Tim around and telling him what to do. On the flip side, I understand that everyone has problems, but I didn't understand why people felt the need to present their problems to me when I had problems of my own. I guess my assignment on earth is to help and support those who look to me as an aide and assist them the best way I can.

I pulled my iPod from my bag, noticing Mr. Marvin looking in his rearview mirror at me. (Let me just say one thing, I have the gift of easily zoning out on people, especially when I'm in deep thought about something.) I was having one of those moments with Mr. Marvin because once I finally realized he was asking me a question, I noticed that I had been ignoring him the entire time. Sometimes I don't even realize that I'm doing it because it happens so naturally.

"You want some McDonald's nephew?" Mr. Marvin continued smiling in his rearview mirror.

"Yes, that'll work." I nodded my head with excitement. That hospital food was the worst and I hated the fact that Aunt Jackie was making me eat everything on the tray, even the dry salads.

"No Marvin, he doesn't need that!" Aunt Jackie turned to look at me. Aunt Jackie sure did know how to rain on somebody's parade. I was on cloud nine just a moment ago and she dropped me back to the ground. "I don't want you eating that mess! I will make you some fried bologna and cheese sandwiches when we get home."

I was still satisfied because I loved Aunt Jackie's fried bologna and cheese sandwiches, plus I knew that Aunt Jackie really cared about my health.

Within seconds later, a light bulb turned on inside my head and I smiled with eagerness. I knew that Aunt Jackie would be overly dramatic while tending to me since I was just in the hospital. I decided to take my chances and be as more dramatic as I could to see how much I could get out of her about Brandon as she tended to me.

"Alrighty then, the first lady has spoken." Mr. Marvin passed by the McDonalds, looking at me with a sympathetic frown.

This trip home was so long, but I wasn't complaining because I didn't have anything to do for once in my life. I just hoped that Aunt Jackie didn't plan on having people come over to see me because I don't like surprises. We were still in the car and I was listening to the music on my iPod. I mean on blast, but not too loud that I didn't notice Aunt Jackie and Mr. Marvin's mouth moving. I turned down the volume, just to see what they were talking about because I felt like I was missing out on the inside scoop.

"I got to go past Veronica's house later on, so I'm going to need you to do the groceries for this month tonight babe." Aunt

Jackie stubbornly pulled out a list with grocery items on it. Mr. Marvin looked as if he wasn't up for it, but as we all know the wife's wish is always the husband's command.

Minutes later, we finally pulled up to the house and seen the neighborhood flooded with police cars and nosy people all around. It was as if the neighborhood complex was corrupted by crime and devastation all of a sudden because it was very clear that something major must've happened while we were gone. Aunt Jackie hates being around police because she always said that they were pain's in the rear end. I always laughed though because every time she would say it, she would scrunch up her nose and roll her eyes real hard. We got out of the car to walk to the steps of the house and in my peripheral, I could see an officer walking up behind us.

"I'm sorry to interrupt you guys, but my name is Officer Cane and I wanted to ask you a few questions." The officer looked serious and very passionate about discovering whatever it was that he was trying to discover. Aunt Jackie froze in place because I told you, she hate police officers. Mr. Marvin stayed outside with her so they could answer the police officer's questions.

"RJ go inside and call Veronica to let her know that I will be there in a minute." Aunt Jackie said as she turned back around to the police officer. I wanted to know what was happening on the outside of the house, but as Aunt Jackie insisted, I went inside to call Cousin Veronica.

"Hello." A raspy voice answered with so much distress and mortification in their tone.

"Hey, is Cousin Veronica there?" I waited with anticipation for a response. Aunt Jackie taught me how to have phone etiquette whenever I called someone's house, even family members.

"She's sleep, can I take a message?" This voice was extremely depressing to me and I didn't know how to continue the conversation.

"No thank you I will call her later, can I have your name?" I asked so that I could give the message back to Aunt Jackie. Before I knew it, the line was disconnected and the person hung up the phone. I put the phone down with so much thought about this voice I heard. It was a feminine voice that I never heard before and in her tone, their seemed to be so much void. Usually I could easily identify voices, especially if it was family, but not this time. It probably was Cousin Veronica's friend or something that came over so they could talk and gossip about the latest news. (My way of thinking is quite interesting, but yet effective because I stick to my thoughts.)

I peeked out the window to see what was going on and I seen Aunt Jackie and Mr. Marvin still talking to the police officer, but this time it was two of them. Their conversation seemed very engaging because everyone, including Aunt Jackie and Mr. Marvin, were laughing and using hand gestures as they talked. I sat down on my favorite couch and picked up the phone to call Tim. Seconds into the call, I got the voicemail instead of him, instantly remembering that his phone was broke. That was a funny, yet embarrassing moment for me because I already knew what was up. I laughed to myself and as I turned the TV on, the phone rang. I looked on the caller ID to see who it was and it read, Veronica Jones. While picking up the phone to answer it, Aunt Jackie and Mr. Marvin walked through the door.

"Hello?" I answered while looking at Aunt Jackie, just to see if her facial expressions changed from the time they were outside, till now.

"RJ, where is Jackie at?" Cousin Veronica asked as she released a sneeze.

As I gave the phone to Aunt Jackie, she gave motion gestures so that she knew who it was on the phone before she answered it. "Its cousin Veronica." I responded to her as I laughed, while passing over the phone.

"Girl he's crazy, wassup?" Aunt Jackie said as she chuckled in silence so that Cousin Veronica couldn't hear her. Mr. Marvin sat on the couch and picked up his newspaper like nothing ever happened outside. I wanted to ask him what was going on, but I was too scared that he wouldn't tell me.

We didn't have that type of relationship where I could ask and tell him anything. It was like I always held back from Mr. Marvin and I don't know why because his conversations with me are usually inviting. The only man that I felt was worthy enough to hear everything that I had to say was my dad and I felt like Mr. Marvin was just trying to fill in the void.

"Mr. Marvin, where is Jaime?" I had been in the hospital for so long it felt like. Mr. Marvin quickly got up and felt his pockets for his keys.

"I have to get her from the daycare in ten minutes and I

forgot all about it, dag!" Aunt Jackie didn't pay him any mind and continued her phone conversation with Cousin Veronica. "You want to go with me RJ?" Mr. Marvin asked as he went to the door.

"No, he needs to rest." Aunt Jackie stopped her conversation to respond to my question. See, just when I think Aunt Jackie's into her phone conversation, she surprisingly proves me wrong. Most females can multi-task though when it comes to engaging in more than one conversation. I honestly think that's how gossiping became so popular because everyone always wants to talk at the same time and have their input.

Mr. Marvin stood up confused as he walked out the door to the car. Another light bulb popped up in my head; Aunt Jackie seemed to be in a great mood and I didn't know what it was that got her feeling good. Maybe it was the cops or maybe it was the conversation that she was having with Cousin Veronica. Since she seemed to be in a good mood, I had to think of a way to get the conversation about my brother back in effect. Plus, I also wanted to know what happened outside with the police. I could not let her stay on the phone with Cousin Veronica the entire time Mr. Marvin was out, so I had to think quick. I looked at her as she continued giggling and thought to myself, 'It's about to go down'.

Chapter Eleven

March 29, 2008

    I was feeling a little unease about things that were taking place in my house. For days and days, Aunt Jackie really had me on watch because of what happened in the hospital. I think what frustrated me the most was when Aunt Jackie would mention to me that she could tell when things were bothering me. She consistently told me that I had to be more expressive when it came to my feelings because it wasn't good to hold things in, as if I didn't know that already. I couldn't express just anything to her because she was the reason I felt the way I did at times. When she got spiritually deep and wanted me to open up and talk, she would tell me that Satan had full access to attack me in whatever way he wanted to. She always went on and on about how Satan was tricky and did things to bring us closer to his trap until he got us. I wouldn't try to listen to her though because first off, it was entirely too deep and secondly, I was trying to eat. Aunt Jackie can be so off at times and I would wonder how we got to random places in our conversations. Aside from that, we never got a chance to cover what we were talking about the night in the hospital because when we had the chance to talk, Aunt Jackie never would mention anything.

    My doctor was forced to prescribe medicated eye drops for me by Aunt Jackie because she had been noticing my eyes getting red too frequently for the last couple of days. Aunt Jackie went to the extreme by getting me a big bottle of Tylenol pills and medicines, just in case I had a headache or something. Aunt Jackie can go over the top with things that are not really serious and these last couple of days was proof of it. Anyway, today was a busy day for me and I knew that I would be cleaning until the dinner tonight at the house.

Aunt Jackie and Mr. Marvin started a new trend in family gatherings, just so that we could all have a good time and enjoy each other's company. It was 4 o' clock and I was still cleaning the house before family and friends arrived. Aunt Jackie invited people from our church, family, coworkers and even people from her high school. I personally didn't see how everyone was gonna fit under one roof because the house was only but so big. I was scared that the neighbors would call the fire marshal on us because of the amount of people we were expecting. Aside from Aunt Jackie's guest, Mr. Marvin had his family and friends as well. I wish I invited Tim, but he was still on the class trip in Italy with the rest of the school.

Prom was next month and I was totally unprepared. I didn't know if Aunt Jackie would let me go because she was always skeptical about school events like prom. I really didn't care about prom because I didn't have a girl to ask. I honestly just wanted to be done with high school and start my future in college.

I continued listening to my iPod, but for some strange reason I could still hear Aunt Jackie talking in the background. I tried turning up the volume, but the volume was up to the max. Mr. Marvin came walking in the door with Jamie in his arms. I could tell she was sleep because there wasn't any movement in her little body.

"Hey neph." Mr. Marvin said while tapping me on my shoulder.

I waved to him as he walked across the room to lay Jamie in her playpen. Everything seemed normal to me and we were like the perfect family. Everyone was in such a good mood, or at least that's what it felt like at the time.

As minutes turned into hours, I slowly realized that Aunt Jackie was beginning to cut all ties. I noticed recently that she didn't really talk to me the way she normally would about things going on in general. Everything was serious now with her and the inside jokes we once had flew out the window. I wanted to blame myself because I felt like I was putting her and the rest of the house through so much. Everything was my fault and I knew that I had to do something about it. I wouldn't be experiencing any of this if my mom were still alive. I could remember when I was younger and how me and Brandon were scared, my mom would pick us up and hold us tight and sing little tunes to soothe our emotions. We loved to hear her sing because of the little rifts she would do at the end of each song she sung. My dad would just smile and rain on her parade by rapping and beat boxing. Those were the fun times that I could remember of my family, my immediate family.

"Mommy, mommy you are my joy." I started to sing the words on my iPod as I went back into thought. Every time I think about my mom, Brandon pop's up and every time I think about Brandon, my mom comes to mind. As I continued cleaning, Aunt Jackie walked over to me and gave me a kiss on my forehead.

"Baby, you are doing a great job with the floor and the dusting." Aunt Jackie said while smiling with sincerity.

"You know I try to do the best I can." I said as I chuckled, hoping that she would chuckle with me. After finishing up with dusting, I put the antique figures back onto the shelf and the glass cross figure on the marble living room table. Mr. Marvin also seemed amazed, but tried not to show it as much as Aunt Jackie did. We really didn't have time to go into depth with the admiration of the work that I did around the house because it was almost time to get the party started. It was 5:33 pm and the family gathering started at 7:00 pm. We had less than two hours to decorate and make sure that everything was in place the way it needed to be. Aunt Jackie was finishing up with the food and Mr. Marvin was finishing up with the little gift bags for guests. I only had a little bit of time to myself so I decided to get dressed early just in case Aunt Jackie or Mr. Marvin wanted me to do something at the last minute.

"Marvin don't stuff those bags too much!" I heard Aunt Jackie yell as I went up stairs.

One and a half hours passed by and it was now 7:10 pm. The church members started coming at first then minutes later, the combined family rushed in. I don't know what happened to Mr. Marvin and Aunt Jackie's coworkers that were supposed to come. I could tell that Aunt Jackie was getting a little discouraged because she really wanted them here at this year's gathering. She would always bring them up and hold many phone conversations with them regarding the family gathering that was taking place.

"Praise the Lord Saints!" Pastor Clay said as he walked through the door while giving people hugs.

First Lady Clay was dressed like she was coming to a banquet. I admired her unique style as I looked at her from top to bottom. Her long and curly hair fell freely, passing her shoulders. The Barbie doll, knee lengthened dress that she had on was decorated with Rhine stones and rubies on the top part and silver sequence that flared out at the bottom of the dress. To put the icing on the cake, she complemented the dress with dark colored lace stockings and red pumps. She was well groomed and as I walked up to give her a hug, the fragrance of her perfume confirmed her refined beauty.

"How are you RJ?" First Lady Clay asked as she gave me a kiss on the cheek.

"I'm fine Lady Clay, how are you?" I was surprised that I was holding an intellectual conversation with Lady Clay and she seemed very interested.

"I can't complain baby, just living." Lady Clay had a smile that had such an influence on me. I felt like living every time she smiled at me. (Now I don't want to sound as if I'm lusting over Lady Clay, it's just that she has a creative way to express herself through her appearance and I really admired it.)

More and more of Mr. Marvin's family members came as the minutes passed and I can honestly say that the gathering came together well. Although many of Aunt Jackie's side of the family weren't in attendance, things still seemed to be going well. I looked around and seen Mr. Marvin interacting with Aunt Jackie's older uncle, Uncle Karl and Aunt Jackie was interacting with Mr. Marvin's mother, Ms. Connie. I loved Ms. Connie because she seemed like she had a great relationship with Mr. Marvin. Families that are close knit are new to me. That's something I didn't have because Aunt Jackie separated me from people that she didn't feel was right for me, including family. She didn't have a relationship with her parents after dropping out of college and was later forced to find her way through life. With no job and no home, Aunt Jackie was left homeless for a couple of months and moved from home to home with some of her close friends families. Cousin Veronica was the only one that reached out to Aunt Jackie once Aunt Jackie revealed everything to her about the dilemma she had with her parents and school. Because I knew that Aunt Jackie didn't have much support at the gathering from family, I wanted to do the unexpected and invite someone that really respected and loved her and that was Lil Rodney.

As everyone continued to enjoy themselves while playing different trivia games Mr. Marvin created and eating the food Aunt Jackie cooked, I stepped outside to run across the street to Lil Rodney's house. Aunt Jackie wasn't paying attention because she was too busy entertaining guests. I walked outside into the cold with no jacket on, but I didn't care though because it was extremely warm inside of the house. While walking across the street to Lil Rodney's house, I looked back at my house and realized that it stood out in the neighborhood. Cars filled the entire block and I could hear gospel music playing throughout the neighborhood. I shook my head and chuckled with gratefulness as I reached the front steps of Lil Rodney's house. I knocked on the door until someone responded and to my surprise, it was Ray. Well, I really wasn't surprised because Ray is always here so I actually expected him to answer the door.

"Sup cuz." Ray said as he opened the door for me to come in.

"I'm alright Ray, is Lil Rodney here?"

I started to get nervous because I felt like I had been outside the house for a while, when in reality I just got across the street to Lil Rodney's house. Ray called Lil Rodney from the back room to come and see what I wanted. I didn't want to get in trouble with Aunt Jackie so I decided to stay and wait for Lil Rodney at the front steps. While waiting for Lil Rodney to come to the front door, Ray would try to hold conversation with me about school and Aunt Jackie. I never knew what type of relationship he wanted to have with Aunt Jackie or if he ever developed a relationship with Aunt Jackie.

"Yo cuz, be safe man." Ray said while taking a puff of his cigarette. "I'm getting a bad vibe from Aunt Jackie man and I don't wanna be feeling this way. It's like every day I'm just thinking about your well being while you living with her, I mean since you my cousin. I'm telling you, I got your back whenever you need me. I know she might tell you otherwise, but everything will soon be revealed to you how she really is and I don't want you to be surprised when it happens."

I zoned out from what it was that Ray was saying because he seemed a little tipsy and high at the same time.

"I got you." I said while noticing Lil Rodney coming out.

"Wassup boy?" Lil Rodney said as he gave me a handshake. I was telling Lil Rodney about the gathering we were having across the street and in my peripheral I could see Ray looking off to the dark sky as if he had lost something so small that meant the most to him.

"I wanted you to come over and support Aunt Jackie, I'm quite sure she will be cool with it." I started to second guess the invitation as I went in depth. I was reminded that Aunt Jackie didn't like surprises and that she would be extremely embarrassed since the church people were there.

"Yeah, I'll come and show my face." Lil Rodney said as he ran inside the house to grab his jacket.

"I wasn't invited cuz?" Ray asked while flicking off his cigarette in the air.

Before I could respond, Lil Rodney had invited Ray to go with him. I began to panic inside because Aunt Jackie didn't seem to really care for Ray and I didn't want any trouble.

"No I was playing Rod, I'm good." Ray said while laughing off his true deep feelings.

Lil Rodney insisted that Ray go with him and I just stood in silence hoping that Ray stuck to his first answer. Ray gave in and went inside to grab his jacket. I waited for Lil Rodney to shut the door and we started walking back over to the festivities. As I opened the door, I noticed that everyone was sitting around the family room in a circle. I could see that Aunt Jackie was pissed for two possible reasons and that was because I left the house without permission and secondly, I had Ray under the same roof. Aunt Jackie never liked to feel uncomfortable in the privacy of her own space. Tension started to rise as Lil Rodney and Ray spoke to the guest at the gathering. Mr. Marvin invited them to make a plate and enjoy themselves, while Aunt Jackie remained silent; smiling uncomfortably. As Ray and Lil Rodney walked to the dining area to grab a plate, Pastor Clay stopped Ray.

"You a family man, I can see it." Pastor Clay started prophesying in the midst of the festivities, which was typically normal at this event. Aunt Jackie should have expected something to happen since she invited the church to her house. "Your life has resulted as a consternation lately, but I want to encourage your heart and tell you that prosperity is about to hit your life and you will fully embrace it with open arms."

Ray started tearing up, like a thug that went to church for the first time. I could tell that the prophesy hit home for Ray and touched his heart as he gave Pastor Clay a hug. As I looked across the room, I noticed people clapping and speaking in tongues as if we were in church. Then I looked at Mr. Marvin and he was smiling, while holding Aunt Jackie as tears consistently ran from her face.

Chapter Twelve

May 21, 2008

Time seemed to be flying by and graduation was a few weeks away. We had graduation rehearsal after school today. My English teacher gave us the task of writing an eight page paper for our final. The instruction for the paper was to elaborate on my high school experiences. In full detail, I had to explain the many lessons that were learned and the benefits that I gained from the experiences. I had to focus really hard and eliminate every distraction that was planted in my mind so that I could finish this paper because I couldn't think of anything that I wanted to write about. I repeatedly looked over the instructions. I grew less and less interested in this assignment the more I read it because I lacked motivation. As I sat at my desk, I began looking around at my classmates, just to see what they were saying in their papers.

"You alright, bud?" Stanley asked while laying his pen on his desk. I think he saw me looking at his paper, but he is cool so I knew he wouldn't snitch. Stan was the class nerd and was very helpful towards his peers when it came to writing assignments in class.

"Stan, I need some motivation so that I could finish my paper before the end of the period." I said while glancing at the clock. I only had forty minutes left to make words magically appear on this paper and perfect it, so I had to think quickly.

"Think about some tragedy or difficult times and problems you experienced while being in high school, then explain how you overcame those obstacles." Stanley said while glancing at my blank papers.

"Stan, you the man!" More and more memories appeared in

my head as I picked up my pen to write. In my first paragraph, I had to have an attention getter so that I would grasp my reader's attention. We learned in class that by doing this, the reader would want to read more.

'I could remember my first day entering high school and being scared of the new faces that I seen. The teachers were entirely intimidating and the work they presented to the class was stressful and difficult. Although school had its hardships, I learned a lot from the experience. One thing that I treasured most about my high school experience was the friendship I gained with my best friend, Tim. Tim has played a major part in my life and I don't really think I would have made it through high school without him. His positive energy and supportive attitude motivated me at the same time as it inspired me. A lot has happened in my life and he was there to step in.'

I started to reflect on our friendship overall and chuckled as I thought about the time Tim and I skipped classes to sleep in at his house during the school day. The ironic thing about every memory I had with Tim was that I usually could remember our stories in full detail unlike the fun memories I had with Aunt Jackie. I continued writing, fully being inspired on what I was writing.

'I felt that Tim filled in the voids of my loneliness from my deceased brother, Brandon. I could remember lunch period during sophomore year when we really got close, Tim would tell me of the many dreams he had of Brandon and in the dream, Brandon passed him a golden torch and placed a golden chain around his neck. Tim would tell me that Brandon gave him the permission to fulfill everything that he didn't have the chance to do with me. Just thinking about it made me realize that I had such a good friend. A motivator and protective friend such as Tim made me appreciate everything more.

As I continued writing, a whirlwind full of thoughts and memories echoed in my brain just like a tornado that passed through a city. "No... Body knows the trouble I see..." "RJ, be careful cuz..." "You're my baby brother and it's nothing that you can do about it..." These thoughts became overwhelming for me, but they helped me even more with my writing. I looked up at the clock and noticed that class was over in three minutes.

'In conclusion, the many hardships that I experienced while being in high school has helped me become a better person.'

I looked over my papers and went up to Mr. Harvard's desk to turn it in. Just as I went up to his desk, the school bell rang, initiating that the school day was over.

"Attention seniors, please remember there will be a

mandatory graduation rehearsal in the school's auditorium today." the intercom spoke loudly through the speakers in the hallways of school.

I walked up to my locker, trying to wait for Tim so that we could meet up and head to the auditorium together. I put my unnecessary books away in the locker and then grabbed my jacket. Minutes had gone by and there was still no sign of Tim, so I started walking to the auditorium.

"Last call for all seniors to be in the auditorium at this time", the intercom made its way through the hallways again. I walked to the auditorium and stood in the very back by the entrance doors. There were so many students and faculty staff that filled the entire auditorium. There were one thousand and two hundred students that were in the graduating class. As I walked through the chaotic crowd of loud students and teachers, I tried looking for Tim.

"Aye RJ, sit with me yo." Lil Rodney said while patting the seat next to him. I was surprised that the school was still allowing him to graduate because of all the days that he missed. I walked over to Lil Rodney, sitting in the seat next to him while looking for Tim at the same time.

"Yo can you believe we doing this?" Lil Rodney asked being a little hype.

I mean, I guess he had a reason to be because he must didn't think he was going to graduate. I tried to be as interested and comfortable in engaging a conversation with him, but at the same time I was trying to look for Tim. "Man, I can." I said while laughing. "It felt like we been in high school forever and I been ready to get my diploma." I said while still trying to spot Tim out.

"Man I feel you because I didn't think I was going to graduate, but they let me." I started to think about how lucky Lil Rodney had been to graduate.

Lil Rodney continued talking, but I was zoning him out because I was still trying to spot Tim out in the crowd. It didn't even hit me to text or call him because things seemed to happen so fast from the time I got out of class. While still engaging in conversation with Lil Rodney, I slowly pulled my cell phone out of my pocket. (Did I mention that I got it fixed? Well its been fixed for some time now, but I forgot to mention it.) I called Tim and it went straight to voicemail. Usually after school, Tim would always hit me up so that we could talk to each other before getting on the bus. I tried texting him and another thing popped in my head.

"His phone is cut off.' I said aloud as Lil Rodney looked at me with a confused face.

"Who you talking about RJ?" Lil Rodney asked as he stood up to straighten up his twisted jeans.

"My homeboy Tim." I said as I noticed Lil Rodney scoping the auditorium.

"Oh, you still cool with Tim?" Lil Rodney asked as if he was surprised about it. He shook his head at me with shame in his eyes, as if he knew something that I didn't. He pulled one of Aunt Jackie's numbers when she would look at me in a mysterious way whenever she knew something I didn't know.

"Yeah, that's my best friend." I started to ask him what was up, but he began speaking before I could get anything else out.

"Man, Ira always talking about you and him and it blows me." Lil Rodney continued shaking his head.

"She doesn't like the fact that ya'll are as close as ya'll are and she told him once that he needs to let you go because something's really wrong with you." As he continued talking, I grew more and more discouraged about the friendship I had with Tim.

"Man, that's crazy. Tim would never listen to her because she seems to be the crazy one!" I was fully confident in knowing that Tim would be my friend until the end.

"Are you sure?" Lil Rodney asked.

I shook my head with so much confidence and I even went into full detail of the things Tim told me about Ira and how she could be controlling at times.

"How do you know Ira?" I asked Lil Rodney as I calmed down, still feeling hurt that she would say something like that about me.

"Oh Ira, that's my home girl, better yet, she like a little sister to me. I used to talk to her cousin Tamra in middle school and since then, we been cool. Now usually I'm not the type to get in niggas business, but since you my peoples too, I'm just gonna tell you to check ya boy." Lil Rodney said while smiling and dapping it up with me.

In the back of my mind, I started to take into consideration everything Lil Rodney was saying to me. At the same time, I started to think about Aunt Jackie and how she would warn me about friendships and how other people can grow to be jealous of connections and friendships I had with people. Since I was growing up and graduating high school, I knew that my way of thinking had to change. For years, my way of thinking was in align with Aunt Jackie's way of thinking. I still was a little skeptical about what it was that Lil Rodney was telling me about my own best friend because I knew Tim more than Lil Rodney did. But at the same time, I gained much respect for Lil Rodney because he was straight to the point with things and warned me, just in case the stories he told me were true; so it wouldn't come as a surprise to me later. The teachers still were trying to get everything together and organized, so I had time to use the bathroom.

"Yo, where you going RJ", Lil Rodney asked while texting on his phone.

"I'll be back, I'm just going to use the bathroom." Dag, Lil Rodney was all up in my personal business. He really didn't chill with a lot of people here at school because he always said they wasn't on his level. Freshman year, I remember Lil Rodney getting into a situation with the Hudson boys who lived around the corner from the school. There youngest brother, Chris went to school with us and they would always come messing with different people just to see how far they could get. One day, Chris tried to confront Lil Rodney about some girl who Lil Rodney was tryna get with. Lil Rodney told him that he didn't have anything to do with Chris' girl, but that she was trying to get with him. From there, animosity and tension between Chris and Lil Rodney grew heavy. Then days later, Chris called for his brother's to meet him after school because he had a problem. They jumped Lil Rodney, but I must admit that Lil Rodney didn't let that situation get to him though because he could have easily transferred like the average young black boy would have if they got beat up at my school. While opening up the bathroom door, my phone vibrated repeatedly. I looked at the ID on my phone and it read, Unknown Caller.

"Hello." I said while looking in the bathroom's mirror to check out my ridiculous features.

The phone instantly disconnected in my ear as I continued saying, hello. I thought to myself, somebody is playing on my phone and I wanted to know who it was. I shoved my phone back into my pocket as I walked up to the urinal. I began releasing the urination from my tool and within seconds, my phone started vibrating again.

"This is crazy yo, who is calling me?" I was frustrated and wanted to drill somebody's face into the ground. I flushed the urinal, pulling my phone back out from my pocket and this time it was a text from Patrick. As I went up to the sink to wash my hands, I opened the text message and it read 'the sky is the limit smh.' (SMH was an abbreviation that stood for shaking my head and it was mostly used when people texted each other in their phones.) I responded to see what Patrick was talking about, but before I could send it, he was calling me.

"Wassup bro?" Patrick said while trying to tame the loud noise in the background.

"Where you at because we need to rap?" Patrick said as my stomach began birthing butterflies uncontrollably.

"What's wrong brother?" I said while holding the phone with my cheek and shoulder so that I could wash my hands.

"I'm just going to say that stuff is real man." I didn't know what Patrick meant but I could tell he was going to explode on somebody in a few minutes.

Chapter Thirteen

May 23, 2008

We were all sitting on the steps on the front porch of Uncle Karl's one bedroom house. It was me, Lil Rodney, Patrick and Ray. Patrick's twin, Eric was away for the weekend with his basketball team. It was the beginning of the weekend. Graduation was in a week and I was excited about everything that was going on all around me again. I forgot that Patrick wanted to talk to me about something because when he would get the chance to talk to me, he would make the conversation about something else. It must wasn't that serious or important, I thought in my mind. I told Aunt Jackie last night that I felt like I could smile freely again and she just smiled at me and gave me a kiss on my forehead. On the flip side of things, I was starting to worry about Tim. I haven't heard from Tim till this day and I started to wonder what was going on with him. I didn't want to believe that it was what Lil Rodney was telling me, but I was slowly but surely starting to. In addition to things, I guess Aunt Jackie started to embrace Ray more because she was receptive to his personality every time he came around with Lil Rodney.

"Yo, stop playing with me!" Ray said to Patrick as he laughed while dapping it up with me. "I would never try to get at her, I mean look at her!"

We were scoping out the dimes from the pennies if you know what I mean. Everyone was outside today and I was starting to feel the summer weather already. Breezy G's Famous Italian Ice store on Third Avenue opened up yesterday and we all were hype because we had to wait an entire year for it to reopen. Uncle Karl lived in the hoodest neighborhood, if that's even a word. We were all used to it though because it was considered home for us. I loved coming around here because it was something going on every time I came around. National recording artists, Fly Boy Rich Kids would come and give live performances at the community center and we would all go. We continued looking at the girls, up and down; back to front.

"Yall drooling over those birds?" Aunt Jackie said as she stood behind the screen door. We all started laughing, pumping Aunt Jackie up to make her feel as though she was *down* like we were.

"Ray come in here for a second." Aunt Jackie said as we all looked at her just to see how serious she was. Ray was cool about it and jumped up from the steps like he had been doing it for years and went inside.

"Yo what you think she wanted?" Patrick asked while eating his favorite Jalapeño chips.

"She probably wanted to introduce him to uncle Karl thoroughly so that Uncle Karl knew that he was my cousin on my dad's side." I couldn't see it any other way.

Ray came back outside smiling as he gave us the signal to come inside with him. We all were asking him what was going on as we piled inside, but he was too busy smiling. As we got inside, Uncle Karl had four plates full of soul food sitting on his dining table. On the side of each plate was everyone's favorite beverage and a golden box. We all went to the table as Aunt Jackie instructed us and sat down in the chairs.

"Wait, don't touch nothing!" Aunt Jackie said as she noticed Mr. Marvin and Jamie coming in from the front door. "Now before you guys eat, we are going to do something a little different that my Uncle Karl would do with me and my friends when I was in my teen years. Its called, *gratitude's attitude* and basically you prepare a meal and a gift that symbolizes what the other persons mean to you." Aunt Jackie went in more depth as I became surprised because I never heard her mention anything like this before to me.

"Before the eating of the meal and the opening of the gift's, the person who prepared everything would express their gratitude with an undeniable attitude for the other person."

We looked around the table, grinning as Mr. Marvin kept taking pictures while we weren't looking.

"Ok so I'll start by saying that you young fella's have helped me on so many level's. Early yesterday morning, I was sitting at the desk at work when a question just hit my mind. The question was, *What does it mean to live with an OPEN HEART?* At first I wasn't too sure because it caught me off guard, then I thought about it. I know that many people may have their own definition for this, but this is what I got out of it and gained from it as well. Many folks in this world are faced with many things, obstacles and situations that usually becomes overwhelming for them. They may become stagnate and experience things that are considered too much and difficult. Sometimes in order for them to get over whatever the case may be, they would have to allow pride to cease and be willing to talk freely without feeling bound by their emotions. It was hard for me to do so at times because I allowed my pride to get in the way. I also didn't speak out when the time was right for me to do so because I always lost thought every time it was time to say something or either I didn't know how to word it when I did have it in mind."

As soon as she made that statement, it hit me that she was tearing down those tough walls that had been in her life for years. I even think that Mr. Marvin was surprised as her husband because she always seemed to be put well together when they were around each other.

"I now realize that in order to live with an open heart, I need to first have the desire to do so." Aunt Jackie began tearing more and more as she talked. I knew that this was something she really took to heart because she never talked around me like this before.

"I know I'm not perfect and I also am aware that I do not know everything, but one thing that I do know is that I am willing to live, learn, love and listen with an open heart. We build and strengthen our character by living with an open heart. There may be a family member or a friend that may need our support and guidance, so we have to be open-minded and look at things from all angles and in every perspective. RJ and family, are you up for the challenge? Who is willing to just listen and accept some things? I don't know about you, but I know that I am ready to LIVE with an open heart." Aunt Jackie wiped the tears from her face while smiling. We all began applauding her, saying that we love her and that she was still the greatest.

"Can I say something?" Ray shouted before we grabbed our forks to dig in the food.

"I promise, I won't be long and our food will not get cold." Ray chuckled as he began transforming to being serious.

"I was jus sitting in Lil Rodney's living room, not too long ago when I was thinking about the people who are in my life and around me, the older ones as well as the younger ones. The ones who smile in my face, but then behind close doors have everything in the world to say. The ones who call me a friend, brother, and maybe even the man of God that I desire to be, then try to degrade me. My intensions are not to be a bad or intimidating individual, but to just get a clear view of the relationships of people that are around me."

Ray kept his eyes on me the entire time while he continued talking. I didn't know we were getting this deep.

"I remember like it was yesterday when I went to church with one of my old friends and his leader, Pastor Hamilton told me that I have to watch who I embraced because it may be people who I am embracing that's not really for me and don't have my interest at heart."

As I glanced at Mr. Marvin, I could tell that he was in tune with what it was that Ray was saying.

"I don't know if someone has ever had a thought such as this, but if so just continue to watch who you embrace because it's gonna bite you in the tail later. That includes conversations too; trust me I had to learn it the hard way. Just like I heard Aunt Jackie say to RJ before, now is the time to evaluate who your friends are. Seriously though and if you feel the need to separate from certain individuals, then do it, stop talking about it."

Ray started raising his voice a little louder than he was originally talking. You could feel the sincerity of his words.

"If you have to worry about, well if I separate from such and such, are they gonna talk about me and try to make it seem like I'm the bad person? I want to tell you, they were never ya real friends to start with. A real friend would understand where you coming from and even if they didn't understand, they would pray for understanding. The time needs to be now when we get all relationships together and get a clear understanding of who people are to us; I love ya'll for real."

As Ray sat down, we could see that he was squinting his eyes to fight back the tears. I never knew that Ray had all of this wisdom in him and I guess it was because I never got a chance to really be around him. Its crazy how the one's who don't really go to church and sit on the corners, smoking their weed and clubbing, be the ones more in tune with God than we who attend church every Sunday. We began applauding again, saying that we love Ray and to continue to be the example that he was. As we began eating, I seen Ray go over to Aunt Jackie to give her a hug. Mr. Marvin didn't miss a moment because he took a picture of that. It felt like a holiday because we had gifts and food and gratitude's attitude. I was pleased with the entire thing. Uncle Karl served us, like he always use to do when we had our family gatherings before Aunt Jackie and Mr. Marvin got married.

"Yo this food good J, shortie can cook." Patrick said to me as we started laughing at our insider about Aunt Jackie. Aunt Jackie first got the name *shortie* when we were like twelve because she would do and say things that reminded us of a young girl.

"I'm use to it." I said while chuckling and eating the remaining meat off of my chicken bone.

Fifteen minutes went by and it was now time for us to open up the golden boxes that were on the side of our plates. Lil Rodney was too anxious like he never received a gift before and Ray was being humbled as if he wasn't ready to even open the gift. Because we been around Aunt Jackie all of our lives, me and Patrick could probably guess what was inside the boxes. As we opened the box, we discovered that each gift was not the same. The dining area was filled with excitement and noise as we held up our opened boxes.

"Thanks so much Aunt Jackie. how did you know I liked this?" Lil Rodney asked while showing his Rolex watch to the three of us. I didn't know where Aunt Jackie got the money to get these gifts, but all I knew was that they weren't the cheap dollar store gifts. She had to spend about a couple thousand on these gifts with the help of Mr. Marvin.

I waited until everyone opened their boxes so that I could open mines. I wanted it to be a special moment when I opened my gift and I didn't want nobody to take my shine; I was being a little selfish. Aunt Jackie got Ray a chained necklace with a cross charm on it and a ring that had his name engraved in it. Ray was overwhelmed and couldn't stop thanking Aunt Jackie.

"That's right, so when all of ya'll get ya jobs, you can pay me back!" Aunt Jackie said as we all laughed while Mr. Marvin took the pictures.

"I'm really proud of ya'll and the decisions that you guys are making as young men. Keep God first and He will have no other choice but to bless you." Mr. Marvin said while removing the camera's eye piece from his eye.

Uncle Karl just kept asking if we wanted more to eat, showing us his hospitality skills. I loved Uncle Karl because he always supported Aunt Jackie even in her worst days. He was considered the baby out of my grandmother's siblings. He would always do for Aunt Jackie and my mom because he always said that they were his two favorite girls. He didn't have any kids, so he went through life doing all of the things that he could do for them. Patrick looked to me, grinning before opening his golden box. As he opened the box, he started cheesing too hard while removing his gifts from the box.

"I got a two hundred dollar gift card from Eddie's Gaming Center, a two hundred dollar gift card from Movies 4 Days, and a thousand dollar gift card from Urban Express clothing store!" Patrick said while looking into the camera to smile with his gifts.

"Let Eric know that I have his gift waiting for him when he returns." Aunt Jackie said while looking at everyone enjoying their gifts.

It was about that time for me to open my golden box from Aunt Jackie. Everybody waited for me to open my box with anticipation, just how I liked it. I opened my box and was astound to find car keys inside. I looked to Aunt Jackie and she shook her head with confirmation while smiling.

"Its outside, I'm surprised you didn't notice it!" Aunt Jackie said as Mr. Marvin took a picture of me holding the keys in my hand. Everybody put their gifts on the table and rushed out side before I could even get out of my seat. I gave Aunt Jackie a hug and could tell that she was holding back her emotions.

"I'm proud of you young man, keep up the good work." Uncle Karl said as he gave me a hug.

Mr. Marvin was already outside taking pictures without me. Before I got to the front porch, my eyes instantly locked eyes with the 2008 black Lexus LS600h as the crew surrounded it in awe. I knew at that very moment that it was about to go down.

Chapter Fourteen

May 25, 2008

    The phone would not stop going off and it was starting to annoy me. I was sitting in my bed room reading my word and studying the book of Revelations in my bible. I wanted to get back to my old ways of reading and praying because things were happening all around me and I couldn't figure out why. My mother would always say that prayer changes things and to stay in the word because it would never steer you wrong. Some things in the bible were interesting to me how descriptive things were and how God thoroughly gave warnings that came to past. Like the story of the lady who God turned into a pillar of salt, literally, and in other scriptures how God gave warnings to the church about His return. These kind of things caught my attention because Pastor Clay would talk about it all the time and preach the church crazy. At times I didn't understand, I would have a mini bible study session with Mr. Marvin when we got home.

    'And I saw an angel come down from heaven, having the

key of the bottomless pit and a great chain in his hand. And he laid hold on the dragon, that old serpent, which is the devil, and Satan, and bound him a thousand years. And cast him into the bottomless pit, and shut him up, and set a seal upon him, that he should deceive the nations no more, till the thousand years should be fulfilled: and after that he must be loosed a little season.'

I was reading Revelation chapter twenty. My mind would not allow my eyes to stray away from what I was reading. As I continued reading, I could hear the front door opening from down stairs.

"RJ come on and get down here so that you can eat boy!" Aunt Jackie yelled as I closed my bible so that I could demolish breakfast.

"Dag, It smells like Aunt Jackie cooked sausage, eggs, ham, pancakes, and fried potatoes." I started guessing as the aroma of food filled my bed room.

It was Sunday morning and we were getting ready to go to church. I looked at myself in the mirror before going down stairs to eat with Aunt Jackie and Mr. Marvin because I had to make sure everything was well put together. Being pleased with what I had on, I smiled as I put on my shoes. I had on a Mickey Mouse crème and yellow colored dress shirt with a crème blazer and striped red bowtie. My pants were a solid yellow color and I had on red and white chucks, just to complete my entire outfit. . (I know that my style seems crazy to the average person, but I like it and that's all that matters.)

I shut my door as I rushed down stairs with my bible in my hand and my new car keys in the other. I was excited to drive to church in my own new car for the first time in a long time. They told me that the car was my early graduation present and that I had one more gift I was going to get at my graduation.

"Well look at you, my nephew fancy!" Aunt Jackie said while smiling at Lil Rodney and Ray. They must was going to church with us because they both had bibles in their hand's and were dressed to impress.

"Wassup Brother Ray and Brother Rodney." I said while dapping them up and laughing.

They were dressed up in full suits with dress shoes and to exaggerate a little, I felt under dressed myself. It caught me off guard because I was not used to seeing them dressed like this. They transformed from baggy jeans and hoodies with fresh Nike's to pinned stripe suits and ties with leather shoes.

"Ok, I see ya'll." Mr. Marvin said while smiling at Lil Rodney and Ray. Ray stood up, smiling from ear to ear as Mr. Marvin checked to see if the suit fit. "Babe, did I do good or what?" Mr. Marvin asked Aunt Jackie while pulling the bottom of Ray's suit jacket.

"Yeah, Ray you really look nice boo." Aunt Jackie said, trying to ignore Mr. Marvin as she put the food onto the table. Ray just laughed while Aunt Jackie and Mr. Marvin went back and forth with their little petty and funny disputes.

"Dag fellas, it look's like round two." Lil Rodney said while pulling out his chair from the dining room table. I was so grateful that everything was starting to come together with my family and family friend, Lil Rodney.

"Hey RJ, have you heard from ya boy?" Lil Rodney asked while putting the fresh cooked blueberry waffles on his plate. I was startled that he asked a question like that at the time we were in front of Aunt Jackie and Mr. Marvin.

"Nah, I haven't talked to Tim in almost weeks!" Thoughts began running through my mind fluently as we engaged more into the conversation.

"It's a funny thing you said that Lil Rodney because I forgot to tell you that he called earlier for you nephew." Aunt Jackie said as she gave Mr. Marvin his plate and orange juice.

"What did he say auntie?" I asked not trying to sound pressed or over concerned.

"He just told me to let you know that he called and to call his home when you had the chance." Aunt Jackie looked surprised, as if it was my fault that she didn't tell me about Tim's call.

I got up from the table and reached for the phone as it laid on the living room's couch. I couldn't believe that Aunt Jackie would forget something like that. I started to wonder and worry even more because my best friend might have needed me. I dialed his number and waited patiently for someone to answer the phone. As the phone began ringing, all I could think about was that I hoped Tim's good. The sound of the answering machine caught my attention.

'Hello and thank you for calling the home of Timothy and Brenda. Because your phone call is important to us, we ask that you would leave your name and number and we will be glad to return your call as the time permits. Thank you and have a blessed day.' I started to second guess if I wanted to leave a message for Tim to return my call, but I just hung the phone up instead.

"What happened baby? Is everything alright?", Aunt Jackie said while walking towards the living room area where I was.

"Yes, it just went to the answering machine, but I guess he will call me back." I felt crazy inside all over again after I thought about the last time we talked. Tim was very pissed at Ira for how she was treating him on the class trip and that is all I could remember. Aunt Jackie stared at me with so much confusion in her face, but she didn't seem to mention anything, although she wanted to.

"I'm going up stairs to get dressed so I could be on time for church, I refuse to be late." Aunt Jackie said while hopping up each step. I went back into the dining area to eat my food with the fellas. They seemed to be done eating their food, but I was fooled once I seen Ray and Lil Rodney making their second plate.

"Come and join us nephew." Mr. Marvin said while reading the Sunday's newspaper. I sat in my chair slowly, putting a little bit of everything on my plate.

"Sooooo let me know something, what's good in the hood?" Mr. Marvin was trying to make conversation with us.

I could always tell whenever he wanted to start conversation because he always would start the same way, it never failed.

"Life Mr. Marvin, sometimes can be so confusing." Ray went on with the conversation as he enticed Mr. Marvin with his elaboration. "Its like you be tryna do the right thing, but something always slips up from under ya feet and keeps you on the same level you've been tryna escape from. I come from a family that really didn't have nothing and RJ you probably wouldn't know this, but when I say I didn't have anything, I didn't have nothing. I always had dreams and goals I wanted to accomplish like graduate high school and go to college, but I ended up hanging with the wrong crowd. My story is not the typical story, although it may sound familiar, but it's a lot to me and I hold it in." Ray began getting emotional as Lil Rodney patted him on the shoulder. "The streets was all I knew, here I am 23 years old with no guidance. I've been a provider for my family for years and no matter how much I supported other people, I never got it back; not even from my own mom and dad. They separated when I was like 15 and she died from AIDS two years later while he was locked up somewhere. I met Lil Rodney through the streets and we been hanging tough every since then. I don't have no family…"

I couldn't believe everything that I was hearing from Ray. I knew that we had a lot of catching up to do since we missed all of these years. Brandon and I really didn't associate with my dad side of the family because my dad didn't either. There was so much pain in Ray's eyes and I knew that this day would be life changing for him. Lil Rodney really didn't know what to do, but to try comforting him.

"Man, I feel you doc." Mr. Marvin said as he passed ray a tissue. "I came from a broken home myself man and it was the complete worst. My dad ran the streets non stop until it killed him. I was the only child he and my mom had and I knew that I couldn't walk in his shoes. In my dad, there was no drive for success or ambition providing for me and my mom…" Mr. Marvin continued as he noticed Aunt Jackie coming down the stairs with Jaime. "I've been from shelter to shelter and lived with people who adopted my family from areas around the ghetto. I know how it feels to struggle and live that life, but we gotta flip the switch and align ourselves with God. As soon as we do that, it's a done deal." Mr. Marvin paused as Aunt Jackie started walking up to his side. "I'm so thankful for my family and my wife man, it's a beautiful thing." Mr. Marvin grabbed Aunt Jackie by the waist.

Tears started to fill Mr. Marvin's eyes, but nothing fell from his face. I looked at Ray and we seemed to lock eyes. I could tell that he really wanted to establish a relationship with me and I was ready. There were so many questions I wanted to ask him and so many things that I wanted to learn from him.

"Ya'll ready?" Aunt Jackie asked as she walked into the kitchen to grab Jaime's baby bag.

We all got up from the table at the same time to throw our plates away. "Ya'll riding with me right?" I asked Lil Rodney and Ray as we picked up our belongings.

"And you know this, mannnnn!" Ray said while chuckling with Lil Rodney. I was starting to feel like I had a family, a real family.

"Auntie, we gonna meet ya'll at the church." I said as we headed out the door waving to Aunt Jackie and Mr. Marvin.

"Be careful nephew." Mr. Marvin said while getting Jaime from Aunt Jackie. "If you do about 80, you should be at the church in no time." Mr. Marvin said as he laughed in Aunt Jackie's serious face.

Chapter Fifteen

When we got to church, it was filled as usual with so many people. It was like there were new faces every Sunday sitting with the visiting ministry team. "I love my church", I said as we stood in the church's vestibule. It was 10:31 am and upper room chamber was crazy. In upper room chamber, the people would pray, seeking change in their situations, problems, etc. As we walked into the sanctuary, one of the elders, Elder Holden stood behind the podium pushing the people to pray and to give thanks unto God.

"Prayer is apart of your worship, prayer serves many purposes in our lives…"

Elder Holden got louder and louder as he prayed. People were falling out to the ground; others were speaking in tongues and crying out loud to God. It was amazing to see everybody on one accord in the spirit of the Holy Ghost. I could tell that Ray and Lil Rodney weren't used to this type of atmosphere because they kept silent and sat in their seats while looking around at the people.

"He said, anything you ask in my name I will do it, anything you ask in my name I will do it. For the prayers of the righteous availeth much, use your power…" Elder Holden continued praying with so much force in his voice.

I stood up while looking around at how prayer impacted the people before praying. I was so glad that things were coming together for the first time in my life and appreciated everything that I was living to see. Although the story of my brother's death remained a mystery and the absence of my father resulted me being fatherless, I still strived for sanity, peace and happiness. I thought about my relationships with others, including my friendship with Tim and how we remained consistent with each other throughout our friendship.

Church to me was not known to be boring or a place that I was forced to come to. Once I really got the chance to understand church for myself, things changed drastically. My way of thinking shifted and I was able to instantly find purpose as I continued being led by God. The sad thing about it is that there are kids my age who still sit in church and don't understand what's going on. Half the time, the majority of them are not trying to really understand because they are too busy being distracted by their lifestyles outside of church. Pastor Clay taught us last Sunday that we shouldn't allow the condiments in life take control of the appetite your destiny hunger's for. Those words have stayed with me and encouraged me to be the best that I could be while having the opportunity to live.

"*He is Lord, he is lord. He has risen from the dead and he is Lord. Every knee shall bow and every tongue confess that Jesus Christ is Lord.*" The praise team began singing slowly as upper room chamber transitioned into morning worship.

More and more people walked into the service as others got up from the ground. The atmosphere of worship never left, but made a much deeper impact on the service. That's what I liked the most about church services at my church. We were not hooked on protocol, but allowed God to move by his spirit and take full control of the service. Lil Rodney tapped me on my shoulder, pointing to Aunt Jackie and Mr. Marvin as they walked in the sanctuary.

"Yo, look at my family coming in." Ray smiled as he stood up to participate in the service.

Minutes went by and it was now time to take our morning offering. I had just got 100 dollars from Aunt Jackie and Mr. Marvin, so I put 10 dollars in my tithing envelope.

"Bring ye all the tithes into the storehouse, that there may be meat in my house, and prove me now herewith, saith the Lord of hosts, if I will not open you the windows of heaven, and pour you out a blessing, that there shall not be enough to receive it." Pastor Clay stood behind the podium with his crisp brown paisley robe on.

"Tithing is simply ten percent of your earnings..." He went on explaining the purpose and the benefits of tithing. I walked to the center aisle with the rest of the tithers. I felt very good about tithing this week because I knew that once I put it on the offering table, I had access to receive blessings and not be cursed by God. Aunt Jackie tried getting Ray and Lil Rodney's attention so that they could join me in the aisle with their tithes. They both shook their heads no, I guess because they were nervous to stand before the church; it was hilarious. Aunt Jackie walked over to them and placed the envelopes in their hands and guided them to the back of the line. I could see her mouth moving fast. At the same time, I noticed them slowly shaking their heads. Pastor Clay led a corporate prayer and then served the people with tithes.

"You will always have seed, in Jesus name." Pastor Clay recited as he shook each person's hand as they laid their tithing envelopes on the offering table. As I reached for the table so that I could place my envelope, Pastor Clay gripped my hand and smiled. "You will always have seed, graduate."

I walked away feeling great and accomplished within myself. While walking to my seat, I tried looking back to see what Pastor Clay was going to say to Ray and Lil Rodney. They had fear in their eyes and could not stop looking at the envelopes they were holding in their hands.

"Well look who it is." Pastor Clay said as he announced how happy he was to see Ray to the church.

"He's a family man ya'll." He began laughing while gripping Ray's hand.

"You will always have seed." Ray walked away giving off a nervous chuckle as Lil Rodney rushed behind him.

Aunt Jackie looked so proud as she stood in her seat, across from where we were sitting. After serving the tithers, Pastor Clay raised the church's general offering.

"Now this is the offering that everyone can participate in, including the tithers." Pastor Clay seemed to be in a happy mood today, but kept looking over at me.

I looked over at first lady as she tried getting her adjutant's attention. She was definitely dressed and I loved the hat she put together with the vintage outfit she had on. I looked at my watch and it was 11:46 a.m. Church seemed to be going by fast, but I wasn't complaining though because I wondered what we were gonna be doing after. I was just happy that Ray and Lil Rodney were here in the service with us.

It was now time to hear the preached word, which I was anticipating from the time we arrived at church. I always got excited about what God was going to give Pastor Clay to say. He was a true example of the man I wanted to be when I grew up. It's his example that gave me the passion to want to read my Bible and pray more consistently.

Pastor Clay walked up to the podium with his bible, notepad and towel just in case he started to sweat on his forehead, I guess. "*We praise thee, oh God! For the son of thy love, for Jesus who died, and is now gone above.*" Pastor Clay began singing as the people stood to their feet to receive him.

"This morning's message will not be of the norm." Pastor Clay warned the congregation.

"This message, I believe will expose you to the greater parts of you and will result in manifestation to the destiny that has been revealed in you."

I knew that service was about to get crazy once I heard the musicians playing high praise music. Pastor Clay started praying as the people loudly shouted from their lungs and clapped their hands.

"And we count it done in the name of the father and of the son and of the Holy Ghost, and the people of God said amen."

Pastor Clay wiped his sweaty forehead. It's crazy because he just got up to preach and within seconds, was already sweating. I looked to Ray and Lil Rodney as they clapped their hands, participating with the people in the church.

"Thank you Lord." I just kept smiling, feeling a great relief and excitement inside of me. I could tell that service was about to go down by the way Pastor Clay started his introductory speech before preaching his sermon.

"Over time, the church or the place of worship rather, has been placed in an era. It has been diagnosed with a disorder that many can't seem to identify. See, in the early days, the temple was a sacred place; it was a place where one came to make sacrifices and lay down burdens…"

I could tell that Pastor Clay had everyone's attention because people responded with a *yes* and *amen*.

"Counseling was available there and rebuke was easily given and received. I'm talking about the temple now, where the spirit of unity; rest, ruled and abided and the *ultimate* focus was lifting up the name of Jesus through praise and through worship."

Pastor Clay continued talking so calmly. "The problem now is that throughout this era of time, where this particular disorder was birthed, the body of Christ stopped exercising discipline. Coming from 1st Corinthians, the fifth chapter, you have a man who had been having an affair with his stepmother; it's about to get good in a minute. Now within the church, the Corinthian believers refused to deal with a specific struggle, so they instantly became naïve and ignored this great tragedy. It amazes me how we have all of these leaders under one roof with a bold and strong personality, which was orchestrated for intersession and discernment, and once the aroma of sin presents itself, we become congested and weak. Now because this was something that the Corinth's could not handle, they felt the need to seek help before the entire church became corrupted and comfortable in their infectious sin. Oh just in case you didn't get the subject today, tell ya neighbor, *I aint come here to get it, I came here with it.*"

Pastor Clay wiped his mouth with his towel. Ray kept me laughing the entire time Pastor Clay started to talk because he would shake his head non stop.

"As I did my study on this, I found something so interesting and fascinating from the great Dr. Hayward Hamilton's theory of sin. He stated that when we adapt to sin, the first step would consist of us getting into an entanglement from a discreet and desirable pleasure. Now within the second step, what we found pleasurable the first time would be considered an unintentional error, bringing us to the third step, which would result in our hidden desires to become arrogant and comfortable lifestyles. It's bad enough that we carry these things, then come to the church to be delivered and healed and end up infecting each other in result." Pastor Clay spoke with so much power behind his voice and I knew he wasn't playing.

"Ask your neighbor, will you heal and sacrifice your infection for me?" The sanctuary filled with praise as the organ hit the high pitch, inviting praise in.

Chapter Sixteen

May 26, 2008

Graduation was on Thursday and I couldn't wait until I walked across that good ole stage. I already planned out my personal dance that I was going to do as I walked across the stage and I knew that I would have people cheering me on as I did it. Today I spent my day with Mr. Marvin, well Uncle Marvin, and my little baby Cousin Jaime. Needless to say, this was going to be a weird day. Mr. Marvin didn't have to work because he had to take care of some church business he told me. He had to prepare for the men ministry's going away trip the middle of next month. I guess he had forgotten about it though because he really didn't talk about it much whenever he could have mentioned it.

On top of that, Mr. Marvin scheduled us to take family pictures at 6pm at The Llaguno Portrait studios on 10th and Lee Avenue downtown. It was 12:35 in the afternoon and we were now on our way to Mr. Marvin's mother, Ms. Connie's apartment. I don't know why this was one on the list of our stops today. Ms. Connie lived in the high rise buildings where the older retired people lived. I wondered how Aunt Jackie's day was going; being as though she went into work today. I could tell she was a little jealous though when she was talking on the phone with Mr. Marvin earlier.

We pulled up at Josephine's High rise center for the elderly in the isolated part of the city. Trees and land surrounded the building while the water fountain made its presence known as people came to the entrance of the building. The security was tight, surrounding the building and the other small areas in this little town. As we parked in the visiting parking lot, I thought about the time Tim took me with him to go see his grand mom. We would go to her high rise building all the time our freshman year and she would have money for us every time we came to see her. Not to mention, skittles because she knew that skittles was our favorite candy.

"Hello and thank you for coming out today, can I have the name of the person you're visiting today?" A little fragile lady said while sitting behind the front desk as we walked into the building.

This was a high class high rise building and I liked it because their seemed to be so much life inside these four walls. On the left wall, I saw the founder's pictures with their biographies. I was surprised to discover that once I touched the picture, a computerized voice read their bio.

"Oh they fancy here", Mr. Marvin said while putting the pen back down on the desk.

"You know, everyone is usually amazed with that picture." The little lady said to me while handling business with Mr. Marvin.

I smiled and continued admiring what I seen around the building. While continuing to look around, a butler came from out of the elevator with Champaign on a tray in his hands.

I never seen anything like this before for old people. It kinda felt like I was in a museum and a hotel at the same time because I thought it was too fancy to be an apartment building. I laughed on our way to the elevators.

"Neph, now don't be shy man when you get up here." Mr. Marvin tried to school me before we got up stairs to Ms. Connie's apartment.

"I'm not, Aunt Jackie was telling me that she was cool, but I already knew that because I was talking to Ms. Connie at the family gathering", I was a tad bit nervous, but tried not to show it around Mr. Marvin. I didn't know what to expect from this visit we had with Ms. Connie today. I remained silent as we got inside of the elevator.

Mr. Marvin kept smiling for some reason, pressing the number 12 button. "Neph I know we don't get out much, but I got something planned for us today man and it's gonna be bangin." Mr. Marvin said while giving Jaime a kiss on the cheek.

As Mr. Marvin continued talking, I was starting to feel weird that he was too excited about spending time with me. I had to remember that he didn't have any son's of his own and because I was the only younger male close to him, he treated me like a son. I didn't want to ever get too close to Mr. Marvin because I knew that one day my dad would come back for me. I felt that if I engaged in a closer relationship with Mr. Marvin, I would neglect my dad and I didn't want that. At this age, I know that I shouldn't be thinking that way, but hey, that's what happens when someone that walked out on you really has your heart. It seems that everyone else pays the price and to be honest, that's what was happening with our relationship.

We got to the 12th floor and made a right down the hall. It smelled weird on this floor, like old spaghetti and air freshener; not a good combination. I looked at Jaime as Mr. Marvin walked in front of me with her in his arms. I tried making a funny face to make her smile, but it didn't work because she just starred at me. We walked up to a bland colored door with the numbers 1212 on it. I took a deep breath as Mr. Marvin knocked repeatedly on the door.

"Where is this lady at?" He said while chuckling as he stopped knocking.

"I'm coming, I'm coming!" I could hear Ms. Connie yelling from the inside of her apartment.

"Well come on then Ms. Connie!" Mr. Marvin said in response to her.

She opened the door and instantly smiled, giving Mr. Marvin a hug and a kiss. They were hugging each other like it's been years since they had seen each other.

"Well hello, Mr. RJ." Ms. Connie said while giving me a hug and a kiss on my cheek. I didn't really think she knew my name because we barely had conversation.

"I'm fine, how are you?" I said while faking my smile.

"I couldn't be any better sweetheart."

Ms. Connie was so nice and it fascinated me because I rarely got the chance to experience people treating me this way. Mr. Marvin walked into the kitchen and into the refrigerator he went.

"Mom, Jaime has everything in her bag that you will need." Mr. Marvin said while pulling out an orange from the refrigerator.

"And if you need me, just call me. Just give me an hour and a half."

An hour and a half? I didn't know what plan Mr. Marvin had up his sleeve and I didn't know what to think. I stood by the entrance of the door feeling nervous because I didn't know what was going on. I looked at Ms. Connie as she was playing with Jaime.

"Alright baby, ya'll have fun!" Ms. Connie said while waving me and Mr. Marvin off.

Mr. Marvin laughed as he gave her a kiss on the cheek and Jaime a kiss. I gave Ms. Connie a hug goodbye, as if I knew what we had planned. Ms. Connie followed us to the door as we were headed to the elevator.

"Nephew, I hope you ready man because it's about to go down!" Mr. Marvin said while putting his arm around my neck as we got on the elevator.

As the elevator let us off at the lobby, all that I could think about was Tim because I still didn't hear from him. Mr. Marvin's cell phone went off interrupting my thoughts. He reached in his pocket for his phone to take his incoming call from I don't know who. I decided to pull out my phone so that I could text Tim. I mean, Tim definitely had my number and I started to think that he was neglecting me.

'Hey my friend, I haven't heard from you in a while man and I'm concerned. Please tell me what's going on with you Negro.' I texted Tim hoping that he would respond to my text message.

We got in the car and pulled off. Mr. Marvin was really into his phone conversation and I could tell that it was with one of the men from the church by the way he was talking.

"I'm on my way to the travel agent right now, just so that I could compare the prices." Mr. Marvin said while turning up the music playing on the radio.

My phone instantly started vibrating with a text notification from Tim. I was surprised that Tim responded and that made me even more confused. I didn't understand why Tim never hit me up before. I guess I had to be the one to initiate everything. I'm telling you, Ira turned that boy out and he was falling right for it. I looked at my phone and opened the notification.

'YO fam... YOU are the reason that everything is the way it is. I'm praying for you're Aunt, your household, every connection you have with others, excluding me now and your life most importantly.'

My stomach filled with butterflies and it felt like my heart was coming out of my mouth. I was extremely confused what it was that Tim was talking about and couldn't seem to piece anything together. I started to reply, but I cancelled the text and put my phone back in my pocket. I started to think, what did I do to deserve this from a boy who I thought was my friend. Ever since Tim came back from Italy, he hasn't been the same and he's been inconsistent in his communication with me. Then I started to think about things that he could possibly be talking about to make him feel like this. Was I holding something from him and he found out or was it really Ira? That fraud is gonna get it, I thought to myself.

 My stomach acids burned the butterflies from inside with fire and my eyes grew heavier as rage ran through my veins. We gonna get to the bottom of this, I thought. I immediately started brainstorming an idea of how to reach out to Tim. I got my car now, so I'm paying home boy a visit when I get back to the crib. One thing you don't do to a person is abuse a friendship and take advantage of their love. I had a feeling that I was about to do something crazy because it was like something was being taken away from me, like in my early childhood years.

Chapter Seventeen

I had gone into this day thinking that I would enjoy my time with Mr. Marvin, but I didn't. Everything seemed forced, from the conversations we had in the car, to the paint ball game we played. That text from Tim really disturbed me. I wasn't in the mood to participate in these activities, but I tried to make the best out of our time.

Me and Mr. Marvin picked Jaime up from Ms. Connie's and was headed to Aunt Jackie's job to pick her up from work. My head was spinning at 100 miles per hour from the thoughts of burning Tim's house on fire. I no longer felt the need to explain myself or even talk to Tim to see where he was coming from because he already had his mind made up. He's an easy and soft nigga and I couldn't believe that he would let a chick get in the way of our friendship. All of that talk he would give me about how he would look out for me since the passing of my brother went out the window. I felt disrespected, hurt and angry all at the same time. My mind couldn't even function properly because his text corrupted it and filled it with pressure building up by the minute.

While me and Mr. Marvin was out earlier, he would try to make conversation with me, but my responses would be short with him. He would then ask if it was something bothering me and I tried to pull the same move that Ray pulled at the breakfast table on Sunday, but it didn't work for me because I couldn't talk straight. All that I kept saying to Mr. Marvin was that I felt disrespected by Tim and that he was an inconsiderate friend. Then every time I would think about the situation as a whole, I would instantly think about Ira without any hesitation. I thought about the things that Lil Rodney told me in the auditorium that day we were in graduation rehearsal and I would get even more pissed just by thinking about it. Mr. Marvin tried to tell me not to worry about it and to now realize that Tim wasn't a true friend to begin with, you know the typical adult talk. But honestly speaking, we are in a different century now and things have changed. With my generation, it's hard to forget about people who you thought had ya back through it all and really cared about ya feelings. How could you forget about that and then have the audacity to put my deceased brother's name in this and try to fill in the voids of my brother's absence. Forget that? Are you serious?

The ride to Aunt Jackie's job was quiet, but I was glad that we had an understanding of how things were at that time. Mr. Marvin knew I was mad and I hoped that Mr. Marvin would just keep driving without asking me questions that would make me even more upset. I knew that in a few minutes, I had to prepare myself for Aunt Jackie and her sarcasm. I really wasn't in the mood to even take the pictures that were scheduled for us, but there wasn't any escaping this one. It was 3:56 pm when I looked at the clock on the radio in the car.

"Nephew, I understand that you're mad, but let's make the best out of the remainder of this day. Honestly, it's like every time we actually have the time to chill and talk, you shut down the moment with other things that blocks the potential we have for our relationship to grow man. I know you and Tim are going through a rough patch in your friendship, but you have to learn to separate how you feel about one person from how you feel about someone else."

Mr. Marvin just served me with wisdom and even though he was right, I really didn't want to hear what he was saying right now. It was one of those situations when you wished you could fly away whenever someone put you in a corner. Reality sucks!

"Mr. Marvin, you don't understand how I'm feeling right now. You may be feeling some type of way about how I am currently acting, but now is not the time to bring your own personal feelings on board."

I think I went a little too hard on Mr. Marvin just a bit. At this point, I couldn't identify his pure feelings from my illusion of his feelings for me. I think that was because he didn't take my side in this situation with Tim. I was so confused about his emotions and feelings regarding me. I didn't give Mr. Marvin any mercy because I was through and could really care less what his response to what I said was going to be. I was prepared for him to go off on me because of the way I responded to his mini lecture, but his response made me nervous.

"Ok." Mr. Marvin said while looking forward on the road.

For the first time in my life, I had given Mr. Marvin a piece of my mind as Aunt Jackie would call it and all he said in response was ok? Now I was totally confused and started to wonder if I mistook the feelings of everyone in my life towards me. I knew that after this, I would have to deal with her next and I was ready because I was in rare form.

Five minutes later, we pulled into Aunt Jackie's office building. Aunt Jackie worked as an accountant for a real estate firm in Upper Haven, near Chestnut Street on the outskirts of downtown. Aunt Jackie killed with the clothes she had on today. People know that they can get sharp when they have prior engagements later in the day. She stood outside with her sunglasses on and her Dolce and Gabbana yellow purse. Mr. Marvin pulled into the handicap parking spot, smiling as he seen Aunt Jackie standing at the entrance of her building. She wore a spring colored yellow ruffled shirt with a lavender half cardigan over top of her shirt. As she walked up to the car taking her time, she let the breeze hit her crème colored balloon pants that had a touch of lavender flower imprints on them. I couldn't see what type of shoes she had on though. Then again, I had to remind myself that I didn't care because I was mad about other stuff going on in my life.

"Hello...Hello...Hello fellas!" Aunt Jackie said as I jumped out of the front seat to get in the back.

"Hey Auntie." I responded, not really wanting to say anything because I wasn't in the mood.

She looked at me like I done something wrong as she removed the sunglasses from her face. Although she looked like she wanted to ask what was wrong with me, she didn't ask and I was happy that she didn't. I could also tell that Mr. Marvin was in his feelings too and tried to put on a show once Aunt Jackie got inside of the car.

"How are you hunny?" Aunt Jackie asked while reaching to the driver side to give Mr. Marvin a kiss.

"I'm better, now that you're here boo!" Mr. Marvin said laughing while staring with lust at Aunt Jackie. He looked like he wanted to rip her into pieces. Aunt Jackie smiled, trying to play everything off like I didn't see the way he was looking at her.

"And how is my favorite girl?" Aunt Jackie said while reaching in the back for Jaime.

Aunt Jackie seemed too happy today. It was like an over the edge type of happy. Something that I had never seen before and it made me wonder if everything was alright. I could always tell when Aunt Jackie was trying to hide something because she would joke too much and even start free style rapping, depending on exactly what it is that she's tryna hide. Or maybe I was looking into her being happy a little too deeply.

"So are ya'll ready to take these pics?" she asked while looking at her image in the mirror of the sun visor.

"Of course baby." Mr. Marvin said as I quietly responded.

Aunt Jackie looked at me through the visor mirror. "What's wrong with you little boy?" Aunt Jackie continued looking at me while I looked out the window.

"I'm good auntie."

I looked at Mr. Marvin as I responded and noticed him shaking his head. It was now 4:32 pm and we had an hour and a half to prepare for pictures. Mr. Marvin kept complaining to Aunt Jackie that whatever we decided to do before taking pictures, he was going home to change his clothes. They then would get in a dispute because Aunt Jackie thought that he brought his clothes with him. I wanted to agree with Mr. Marvin, but I kept quiet instead because I really didn't care about taking pictures. As I spent more and more time in this car, I would become irritated by little things. *Ding-Ding-Da-Da... Ding-Ding-Da-Da;* Aunt Jackie's ringtone on her phone made me want to pick it up and throw it out of the window. I was at my peak with everything and couldn't wait to go home so that I could handle what I wanted to handle with Tim. We got back onto the highway after driving through the city so that Mr. Marvin could get his clothes for the family portraits.

"Yeah girl." Aunt Jackie said rushing to answer her phone.

I closed my eyes, dreaming that I was in another place other than this car with the two of these people.

"Ahaahaha... You are a fool hussy!" Aunt Jackie laughed loudly while glancing at Mr. Marvin as he continued driving. "I'm going to call you when I'm done with everything that I have to do today." Aunt Jackie said while chuckling in her high pitch tone. She got off of the phone and completely interrupted the peaceful mood that was once in the car before she got off the phone. "Babe, you wouldn't believe what Veronica told me." She went on explaining her conversation to Mr. Marvin.

As my eyes remained closed, my teeth clinched together and my hands began to form a fist. Within seconds, it started to feel as though we were on the road for hours and it had gotten to the point of being uncomfortable for all of us. Aunt Jackie seemed to develop an attitude as she sat in the front seat with her arms folded while Mr. Marvin continued driving with tension in his eyes.

"So what are you gonna do Jackie?" Mr. Marvin said as he looked over to the passenger side at Aunt Jackie.

"What you mean Marvin, I'm not gonna choose between you and my nephew, the hell I look like?" I could hear Aunt Jackie talking as I slowly opened my eyes without them noticing me wake up.

"I'm not gonna take any disrespect from a young boy that I'm consistently tryna look after man, I'm not!" Mr. Marvin's voice grew more and more intense as he talked.

"Nigga you aint my daddy and you will never get in between me and my aunt!" I interrupted Aunt Jackie before she could continue the conversation with him. She was surprised that I began talking because I was sleep during most of their conversation. "So what you gon' do homie?" I felt the hood from my dad's side of the family coming out on this church boy and I didn't care. Aunt Jackie tried telling me to shut up, but I was too distracted with the argument that me and Mr. Marvin was getting into.

"Continue acting like that and you will be removed from my house lil man, believe dat!"

Mr. Marvin tried to bring out his hood I guess. Before I knew it, I reached to the front of the driver side and connected my fist to Mr. Marvin's jaw. We began fighting while he was still driving, not really taking his left hand off the steering wheel. All I knew was that I continued banging my fist to his face like I was knocking on a door trying to get inside.

"RJ, Stop you disrespectful little bastard!" Aunt Jackie repeatedly yelled while trying to get me off of Mr. Marvin.

"Nigga you wish you was me that's why ya'll marriage miserable, you cunt!" I continued yelling out while rocking his jaw.

Mr. Marvin slammed on the breaks, tryna pull over to the side of the road.

"Get the hell out of my car and I mean that, you disrespectful orphan!" Mr. Marvin yelled as Jaime began crying in her car seat.

I couldn't believe that Mr. Marvin called me an orphan and I think that really made me act like a chaotic fool as if I was fighting for my life.

"Stop you bastards!" Aunt Jackie screamed from the top of her lungs while slapping me and Mr. Marvin in the face. She pulled me off of Mr. Marvin, punching me in my arm.

"I got you my nigga!" I said while smiling and gasping for air at the same time.

Jaime continued screaming uncontrollably as Aunt Jackie began to breathe heavily out of exhaustion while reaching in the back of the car to pick up Jaime.

"RJ, put that pacifier in Jaime's mouth please. We're almost here." Aunt Jackie said.

I woke up from my dream, realizing that we still didn't reach the portrait studio. Still half sleep, I reached for the pacifier in Jaime's car seat and put it in her mouth. I then pulled my phone out of my pocket to see if I missed any calls or text messages. I realized that I had three new text message notifications back to back. I opened up the new text messages and seen that I had two from Patrick and one from Mr. Marvin. I couldnt understand why Mr. Marvin would send me a text message and we were in the same car. I decided to read Patrick's text messages.

'Hey bro, what you doing?' Was the first text I seen before moving on to the next text message from him.

'Yo, we need to chill man... All of us... You, me, Ray, Lil Rodney, Eric and TIM so we could all have that nigga chat lol!' I laughed while reading that text as I hit the button to respond to Patrick's text message.

'Lol you a nut bro... The fam about to take some family pictures at this place, but I don't know if that will be a good idea. Me and Tim aint cool no more... I don't know why, but that's what he told me. I wouldn't mind chilling with the rest of ya'll though. Maybe we could go to Tim's crib and show him up lol.' I responded while laughing.

Mr. Marvin kept looking back to me as if he wanted to say something. That dream had me looking at him completely differently now. You know how it is when you have a dream and when you realize it was a dream, it still has an effect on you? My phone vibrated again, just as I was about to open up the text from that fool in the front seat, Mr. Marvin.

'Man, it can't be that deep yo lol... Ya'll just going through like real boy's do.' Patrick responded as I noticed us pulling up to Llaguno's Portrait Studios.

'Lol yeah I guess man, we gonna see.' I responded while smelling the fragrance of Aunt Jackie's perfume being sprayed onto her body.

"Nephew, you ready to smile?" Aunt Jackie asked while putting her perfume back into her purse.

"I guess so auntie." I looked at Mr. Marvin as I noticed him looking back at me. The way he looked at me reminded me that he sent a text message that I didn't check. I wonder what this nigga wanted, I thought to myself, feeling crazy that he would even consider sending me a text like we were really cool.

'Nephew, I have nothing but love for you boy. We gonna get this right between us and I will do whatever it takes to make that happen. -Uncle Marvin.'

I was rather shocked that Mr. Marvin sent me a sentimental text and still wanted to establish a relationship with me as his nephew although I brushed him off. I looked to him before getting out of the car and smiled to him discreetly before Aunt Jackie noticed. Mr. Marvin responded by shaking his head and putting his thumb up in the air. From that point on, I knew that things were going to be alright between Mr. Marvin and I.

Chapter Eighteen

May 27, 2008

    I was starting to really see things for what they were. It was 7:05 the next morning and I was feeling a lot better than I did yesterday. I woke up feeling inspired by the text message Mr. Marvin sent me yesterday in the car. My inspiration lead me to the thought of compromising and working things out with Tim, even if he didn't want to hear anything that I had to say. As I laid in my bed, I could hear Mr. Marvin getting in the shower before getting dressed for work. His humming was loud and not put together, messing up the peaceful mood in the house. Aside from that, I no longer had to go to school, which I was extremely happy about, but on the other side of it, I was bored out of my mind.

    Graduation was two days away and I rarely heard Aunt Jackie talking about it. I knew that she knew about it and I also knew that Mr. Marvin knew as well. However, the two of them never seemed to make mention of it though. Maybe it was because there was so much going on this weekend and the other days that caused them not to talk about it. I'm really not making a big deal of it, but I wanted them to understand that it would only be right to encourage me as I entered a new level of success in a couple of days. Ugh, I hate being woke out of my sleep because it's hard to get back to dream land once reality corrupts. In addition, I never knew how much laying in the bed could get my mind flowing and thinking things that I would never think about before. Whether it dealt with past stuff or maybe even fantasies, all that I knew was that I wanted today to be different. I had free time on my hands and I was able to drive anywhere since I had my car. I thought about inviting Patrick and Eric's cousin, Gina over. Sleepy dust hit my eyes all of a sudden as I thought about how Patrick was telling me the other day that Gina was diggin' me and wanted to get to know me.

I met Gina one day when me and Patrick went to the mall to get his little sister Kailyn a birthday gift for her surprise party. Before we pulled off, Gina would try to cling to Patrick as if she was his favorite cousin, but she was using all of that to get my attention. Its funny how girls act, just to get the attention of a dude that they like. *Knock… Knock* I could hear the sound of Aunt Jackie's knuckles against my door. Usually, she would just walk in my room without knocking, but today was different.

"Nephew, I need you to do me a favor." Aunt Jackie said as she shut my room door behind her. Aunt Jackie never really asked for favors, especially for me to fulfill. Because I loved Aunt Jackie it was difficult to say no, so you know I did it.

"Yes Auntie." I said as I noticed her pulling out a piece of paper from her robe with a number on it.

"You know that auntie loves you and would never let anyone do anything to you, right?" Aunt Jackie was starting to scare me and I didn't know what she was about to say out of her mouth.

"Of course auntie, what do you need me to do?" I asked while stumbling over my words.

"Ray is planning a surprise for you to link up with your dad, but according to the state of law, he is not permitted to see you. I need you to hear me carefully and understand that I'm not tryna stir you in the wrong direction, but I need you to call this number if that happens."

As Aunt Jackie handed me the paper with the number, I was afraid to ask her anything else. I really would like to see my dad, but I don't want it to become an uncomfortable thing for me or my Aunt Jackie. I started to think about the night Ray was high and grooving when I invited him and Lil Rodney to our family gathering. He told me that Aunt Jackie was a mystery disguised and that I would learn her motives eventually. I would never feed into it though because nobody couldn't tell me about my Aunt Jackie more than I could.

"Well what number is this?" I asked, hoping that she would tell me before I got too carried away with what she wanted me to do.

"It's his parole officer, Officer Paul." Aunt Jackie handed me the paper while shaking. I never saw Aunt Jackie look so stressed and I didn't understand what was really going on.

"Auntie, how did you know that Ray was planning this?" I wanted to know everything that she did, especially if it concerned me doing something that I was not comfortable doing.

"Well nephew, me and Mr. Marvin were talking and Marvin told me that today would be the day you would meet your father because of what Ray had planned." Aunt Jackie began crying. I still didn't understand Aunt Jackie's emotions, but I knew that this was affecting her something serious.

"I told Marvin just like I told you, it's forbidden by the state for him to see you. I should have told Ray not to consider making that happen because of these things, but its nobody's business." Aunt Jackie stood up from the bed while shaking her head. She began singing her song, "*No... Body knows the trouble I see, nobody knows but me*".

I knew that there was more to this, but I couldn't get my hands on it. It seemed like every time Aunt Jackie would hear my dad's name she would crouch up and act all crazy. She must have had a strong hate for him because of what he did to my mother.

"Ok ok ok Auntie." I said while laying the piece of paper on my night stand. Aunt Jackie's face cleared up from the tears that ran from her eyes.

"Nephew thank you so much, I think we jumped into embracing Ray extremely too fast because he's getting into things that he's not supposed to be getting into. It breaks my heart, knowing that you are growing up and have been unaware to some things that I as a guardian have been protecting you from. Your father neglected you and ran off with Brandon because he knew you were a mommy's boy and also knew that Brandon was a daddy's boy. It's a shame what ya'll kids had to go through." Aunt Jackie sat back onto the bed and gave me a hug just like she did in my younger years.

"Baby, you're special and God is going to use you and make you spiritually bold to tear down the walls of the enemy. The power is in your mouth and the anointing is on your life." those same words she said to me when I was a child was said to me again. "RJ, live life to the fullest." Aunt Jackie smiled and gave me another kiss.

I woke up, gasping as I jumped up from my bed. I didn't hear a sound coming from outside of my room. I was too scared to get up because I didn't want nothing to be on the other side of that door once I opened it.

"The blood of Jesus." I kept saying as I got up to open my bedroom door. As I opened the door, I looked in the hallway and noticed that everybody was gone to work.

It was 2:21 in the afternoon and I needed to get dressed so that I could get out of the house. I walked downstairs in my white beater and boxers, tryna see if the mail came. I noticed a big pile of mail envelopes on the floor and some advertisement papers, included in the pile. All of the mail had Mr. Marvin's name on it, so I just threw everything back onto the floor. I rushed up the stairs, getting my clothes out and feeling swagalicious. I pulled out my khaki shorts with a brown graphic t shirt and my brown chucks to wear on my feet. By the time I ran the shower water, I had forgotten half of the dream that I had earlier about Aunt Jackie. 'Oh well, it wasn't that deep' was all that I could think at the time because I knew that it wasn't something to look forward to. One thing I noticed differently about today than any other day was the lack of incoming calls or text messages from Ray and Lil Rodney.

"Those nigga's probably sleep." I said while taking off my underwear to get in the shower.

As the water hit my body, I started to think about Gina again. This time, it was starting to get intense because I knew that it would be easy for us to get together. See, my fantasies were no longer fantasies because I knew that they had the potential to be birthed into a reality. My pipe started to get stiff as my heart began racing while thinking about her.

"Yeah, that's wifey right there." I convinced myself that I would get her.

Chapter Nineteen

The day was passing right before my eyes. My watch read 6:07 pm as I looked down at it while waiting for Ray and Lil Rodney to get their food out the Chinese store. I noticed that I had been texting Gina since I got dressed and left the house earlier today. She had me open like a can of sardines with crackers and kool aid. I wanted to play it smooth though and not get my hopes up because I didn't want to move in too fast and have her thinking I was easy. My cell phone ringing distracted my thoughts. It continued going off as I hit the answer key.

"Nephew, they found the family!" Aunt Jackie screamed in excitement.

"They found the family who killed your brother and locked them up!" I was relieved at that point because I knew that things were coming together and that my questions were getting answered as the days went by.

"That's good auntie, how did they catch them?" I asked as I noticed Ray playing around, punching Lil Rodney in the Chinese store.

"Baby, they tried to hideout at a motel and left all the information on the table in their house as if the cops wouldn't get to it. Apparently, they put six ecstasy pills in your brother's food one evening after he got into it with his foster mother. The article said that moments after, he died instantly and police found his body wrapped up in the basement of their home. Neighbors had been complaining that they seen a large amount of flies on the windows inside of the house and that nobody had been home."

Aunt Jackie got more dramatic as she told me what she read. "The newspaper really got detailed with this story, but they are giving his foster mother, Gloria Gates ten years with no bail and her other kids are now with the state."

I started to tear up as Aunt Jackie chuckled to herself. I thought to myself, that's no way to kill a child, even if they had been arguing. My world turned upside down at that very moment. I grew more hatred towards my dad for straying away from Brandon and leaving him abandoned with people that he didn't even know. I thought about the many stories that Aunt Jackie told me as a kid about my brother and how my dad molested Brandon. I didn't think it was true though because other things were coming out in the papers and being revealed to me, just like I thought that my dad had another family according to Aunt Jackie.

"Oh wow, auntie give me a second and I'm gonna call you back." I said as I noticed Ray and Lil Rodney picking up the bags from the counter. I had to clear my mind within seconds before they noticed a change in my emotions. I hung up the phone and wiped my face from excess tears that filled my eyes. Ray and Lil Rodney rushed out the store, laughing and joking around with each other as they got into the car.

"Man, you a knuckle head son." Lil Rodney said to Ray as they pulled their phones out at the same time.

"Nigga, you wish you was like me." Ray responded while laughing. "Yo, you good cuzzo?" Ray asked while he put his phone to his ear. I didn't know how to respond to his question without giving my emotions away.

"Yeah, yeah I'm good cousin." I said while clearing my throat.

The car got quiet as I remained speechless. I made plans to go chill with Gina later on tonight, but I instantly lost all desire to do so. Brandon was running heavy on my mind and the fact that Gloria Gates killed him the way she did blew my mind, times a million. I started to think differently and loose respect for my morals in being considered the nice guy. Aunt Jackie raised a young man that's respectful and responsible when it comes to many things, but I felt myself slowly turning into a monster. A monster that prioritized revenge as first in their life and pain and strife as the chicks on the side. I had lost respect for the people that I once cared most for and didn't care too much about the remaining ones who were left. Imagine me, what the hell I look like being a care giver to wolves in sheep's clothing. Imagine me, I'm an innocent young boy that's been trapped by deceit and torment. I see kid's everyday with things they could easily treasure and value. However, when it comes to me, I'm always being sheltered from potential and overshadowed by the very things close to me. I mean, come on and take the time to imagine me. I felt like I was in this world alone because my support wasn't really visible. It was like everyone was slowly disappearing on me and I couldn't figure out how to make them reappear. I felt that if I expressed how I was feeling by my actions, everything would change for the better.

"Yo, shortie got back and needs to let me get some of dat action!" Lil Rodney yelled out while pointing out some random girl walking down the street.

These two knuckle heads wanted to go out to the club for me and Lil Rodney's graduation, but because they know how Aunt Jackie was about curfew, they decided that we all go to this car show. I really wasn't feeling it though, but just to get things off my mind temporarily, I decided to go on with the plans. We had to pick up Patrick and Eric from their crib and then we were on our way. This would have been a good time for Tim to come along with us, but ya'll know how he acting by the text message he sent me. Not to mention, he was apparently too wrapped up in Ira's toxic love to do anything normal. I really developed an urge to confront him over the past couple of days but never had the chance to do it because Aunt Jackie always kept me preoccupied.

"Yo RJ, Aunt Jackie really getting in the way of our original plans man." Ray said while drinking his home made tea that he got from the Chinese store.

"Man don't sweat it cuz, I'm telling you after I graduate and get my diploma, it's a wrap for that house."

I felt freedom come up from my mouth and to be honest, it was a good feeling. Even Ray and Lil Rodney was surprised that I responded the way I did because they wasn't used to me talking like that. With all due respect, I love and appreciate the valuable lesson's that Aunt Jackie taught me growing up, but I needed to learn some things for myself or I was going to be one lost individual. I picked up my phone so that I could hit Patrick and Eric up just to tell them that I was on my way to get them. I lied to Aunt Jackie earlier though because I told her that I was going over to Tim's house for the day to chill and would be back home around one in the morning; once I got done helping him and his dad with their project in the garage. I knew that it was a lie, but Aunt Jackie would believe anything that I told her, especially if it involved Tim. I didn't tell her that I would be with Ray or Lil Rodney because she didn't really want me getting too close to them. She told me that in order to be around them, she would have to be in the equation because it's safer when she's around. We pulled up to Patrick and Eric's crib, listening to Fly Boy Rich Kid's CD.

"We gettin' it in! We getting' it in!" Ray and Lil Rodney screamed out while throwing their fist in the air.

I honked the horn so that they knew I was outside. My phone started to vibrate with a text message notification from Aunt Jackie. As I looked at the text message, I shook my head with devastation.

Nephew, what's up with this letter from your dad that I found under your mattress?

I knew that if I didn't respond, she would call me; I had to think of something quick.

'I had that stored from a while back when Tim and I went to my mom's grave site. I seen the letter sitting next to her grave stone so I read it and kept it to myself.' I didn't know if that was the right thing to say to Aunt Jackie because she was crazy, I'm talking loco.

Patrick and Eric both came out with matching fitted caps on their head. At this point, nothing was settling with me because I lied to Aunt Jackie. I was told some disturbing news earlier and still wasn't at mends with my best friend. I felt like jumping off a bridge and hitting my head on the ocean's bottom. 'I'm always the blame, no matter how hard I try.' I began thinking the worst in my head because that's what things felt like. I never had a chance to tell my side of the story, nor did I ever have the freedom to make my own decisions.

"Wassup Fein boys?" Patrick said as he and Eric jumped in the car dapping everybody up. Ray was hype to see them coming with us because he liked going out in packs, just in case something popped off.

"Wassup RJ? I'm surprised my God mom let you out the house boy!" Eric said while laughing with the rest of the crew.

"We said the same thing cuz." Ray said as he began rolling

up his weed.

Usually, I get a little uncomfortable when stuff like that happens around me, but today was different. As I continued driving, I was starting to feel a little light headed by the smell of the weed. Maybe I was catching contact and didn't know I was. All of my worries were slowly leaving my skull and I was feeling good about everything. Aunt Jackie didn't even respond to my text message and I could care less if she did. As we pulled up to the car show, the lot was packed with madd nigga's and free lanced looking chicks. By the time we parked, we were grooving and feeling good. Ray shared his blunt with Lil Rodney, Eric and Patrick. I only took about two pulls, plus I caught contact. Everything seemed to be funny to us when we got out the car, like this chick that tripped over her two feet.

"Shortie over here tryna step in the name of love." Lil Rodney said while demonstrating his shuffle dance.

We all started laughing, hyping up his joke on home girl. I think she heard us too because she looked back and stuck up her middle finger at us.

"I still love you though, ma!" Ray was feeling good and I could tell by the way he was approaching females and mean muggin' the nigga's.

I love money...I need bread... Money over chicks is my motto, well said' Lil Rodney's ringtone on his cell phone instantly went off, interrupting our laughing moment.

"Hello?" I could tell that Lil Rodney was a little hesitant to answer the phone by the way he answered it. Ray paused what he was doing and looked at me as if I was the one on the phone.

"Yeah pops, I got you." Lil Rodney's voice changed as his posture became unease. He hung up the phone and put it in his pocket.

"Aye yo, my pops brought my grand mom to move in with us since she has a few days to live." Lil Rodney told Ray as he began shutting down.

"Aight, that's cool cuz." Ray said, brushing his real feelings to the side.

"I don't mean to tell ya business homie, but we all family. You gotta find another place to sleep my nigga." Lil Rodney said while looking down at his phone.

I looked to Ray and noticed him slowly loosing his high as

he began to ponder on what Lil Rodney told him. I knew that I would have to think of something quick because Ray didn't have anybody but us.

"Let me call Aunt Jackie to see if it's cool with Mr. Marvin for you to stay with us." I felt bad and didn't want to see my cousin homeless. Patrick and Eric didn't know how to react to what was going on because they were still grooving off of their high, not really comprehending.

"I appreciate dat cuz, if not I guess I can go to the 24 hour shelter on Columbus Boulevard near ya'll house."

Chapter Twenty

May 28, 2008

So everything worked out last night with Ray staying with us. I had to make up another lie to Aunt Jackie, just so that he could stay with us. No I take that back, I just told Aunt Jackie the truth about Lil Rodney's grandmother moving in with them. It was obvious that Lil Rodney didn't tell his dad Ray had been staying there with him though because Ray was forced to leave out of respect for Lil Rodney and his obedience to his dad. Aunt Jackie really didn't want to accept my plea because she said that it really wasn't our problem, but because Mr. Marvin is the type of man he is, Ray was accepted with open arms. The only thing was that he had to find a job by the middle of next month and also try to help out with things at the church. I knew that eventually, they would drag me along with their deal because Ray wouldn't want to go by himself.

Graduation was tomorrow. Because Ray moved in with us, it caused Aunt Jackie to go back to her old ways I guess. She always goes by the saying that it's a lot different to have a relationship with someone, then have them move into your personal space. I guess that Aunt Jackie was showing Ray love from a distance, not ever thinking that he would eventually move in with us. It's crazy how God does things, but oh well. I calmed down a little and felt better than I did before. I started to get in the habit of smoking with Ray while Aunt Jackie and Mr. Marvin were at work and I must say that it calms me down all the way; Lord please forgive me. But for real though, Ray was becoming a close friend of mine although he was a cousin too.

It was 10:31 in the morning and we were up early, chilling

on the backyard smoking. I would think that Ray had more respect than to smoke at a Holy Ghost filled house, but he became too comfortable with everyone. Aunt Jackie told us that she would be getting off of work a little late because it was always busy on Wednesdays, plus she was leaving work early tomorrow for my graduation day. She finally mentioned graduation without mentioning how she felt about me graduating. I mean, at least she remembered that it was tomorrow. She also mentioned that she wanted to talk to me when she got off of work. I hated having talks with Aunt Jackie because I always knew that something was up. I could hear the house phone ring from inside the house, but I didn't bother to go and answer it. The phone rang again and this time, I made up my mind to answer it.

"Hello, who dis?" I said as I let out a cough.

"It's your Uncle Karl son, where my niece at?" Uncle Karl was like a prophet because he always knew when I was doing something wrong or the people I hung around were in mess. I tell you, church people know how to knock the mood down a couple of notches.

"She's at work Uncle Karl, you need something?" I asked, trying to get him off the phone.

"When she get's there, tell her that I need her to call me. Your cousin Veronica called me up and told me that Jackie's been feeling uneasy about that boy ya'll let stay there. Now I don't know him all too well and I know that he's ya kin, but he is trouble, ya hear me son?"

Uncle Karl went on and on about how my dad side of the family were no good and how back in the day, my mom would come to him about their arguments.

"I don't care if she's at work or not, tell her to call me now and if I don't hear back from her in the next ten minutes, I'm coming to the house myself and all hell gone break loose." I didn't know that it was a problem for my cousin to stay here with us after Mr. Marvin told him that he could.

"Aight, Aight Uncle Karl." I hung the phone up in his ear.

I was starting to tense up a little because after all of that crying Aunt Jackie did in expressing her emotions to this boy, she had the audacity to turn people against him and make him seem like an evil person. Ray came inside, yawning as he sat down on the couch in the living room.

"Cuz, who was dat?" Ray asked as he turned the TV on to watch the dvd that was in the dvd player from last night.

"Oh, that was my Uncle Karl, you remember when we had that dinner at his house?" I tried to get Ray to remember who he was.

"Yeah, yeah I remember him; He was a decent man." Ray began speaking highly of him and how he treated us when we were at his crib.

I never knew that Uncle Karl had some mean blood in him though. As me and Ray continued talking, a thought came to mind that I had never thought about before.

"Cuz, I know that this may be weird asking you this, but do you know where my dad is?" I was so anxious to hear Ray's response.

"Yo on a real, I think ya dad still in the pin cuz." Ray said while looking at his phone.

"Then again, he might be out though because I remember seeing him talking to ya Aunt Jackie a while back before the reunion at this restaurant on Spruce Street, near the bowling alley. Yeah, It's coming back to me now." Ray continued talking, looking into outer space. (Now ya'll know that the truth comes out when people are either high or drunk).

"Yeah and when I went over to speak to him, your Aunt grilled me, like who are you? This had to be four years ago because ya dad had just got out of jail then. But yeah man, when I had seen them together, it looked like they were discussing some important business, but then again I can't remember everything because that was in '04." Ray stopped talking as he noticed my fist balling up.

I was hearing too many stories and didn't know who to believe because things weren't adding up. The many talks that Aunt Jackie had with me were no longer making any sense and I was starting to believe that she was living a lie. I felt like doing damage to the next thing that didn't agree with what I wanted to do. I'm talking serious damage, like damage that I would probably regret. The phone began to ring again. I saw on the caller ID that it was Aunt Jackie calling from her job.

"Yeah." I answered with a nonchalant attitude.

"I was trying to hold this until I got off of work, but things aint sitting right with me while I'm here at work." Aunt Jackie began moping over the phone. "Ray needs to leave by tomorrow because we really don't know him like that, plus we barely have any room." She went on without giving a valid excuse.

"Marvin was complaining last night how things seemed weird ever since he got here, now I'm sorry but we're gonna have to figure out something."

I got more intense because I felt like they were being phony the entire time Ray started coming around. Why express that now once you openly invited him into the house?

"Aunt Jackie, I dont know what to tell you, but I guess ya'll can do what ever ya'll gonna do when ya'll get here." I hung up the phone in Aunt Jackie's ear.

I really didn't care because I now viewed her and Mr. Marvin as some cowards and even Cousin Veronica too. She loves to gossip when in all actuality, her house ain't altogether. I slammed the phone back on the hook and began yelling from the top of my lungs.

"These fools don't love me, they phony nigga's!" I said while kicking the couch.

Ray was confused as to what was going on and I didn't really feel right telling him. At the same time, I didn't want to no longer hold my emotions in because they have been bottled in for too long. Within seconds, I instantly went on a rage in the house, punching holes in the walls and breaking the coffee table that sat in the center of the living room.

"Yo calm down cuz, whats ya problem my nigga?" Ray asked while holding my arms.

"Nigga get off of me before I kill you, I'm tired of being lied to and not knowing what's going on with this family!"

I could feel my heart racing as pulses from every part of my body started jumping.

"Ray let me go!" I said as I noticed him following after me to see what I would do next; it was a rap after that.

All I knew was that I had a knife in my hand and was walking towards the living room with it. I jabbed a deep cut into the furnished sofa that was in the living room and carved, *imagine me* on each side of the wall. *Imagine me* was something that I lived by. It was an outlet for my well being and also a stress reliever. People don't know what goes on in this little mind of mine, but once they see the result of what I've done, they instantly catch on to my emotions because they see, *imagine me* on everything I destroy.

"Yo cuz, do you know what you doing man? You are jeopardizing everything man and it's not a good look!"

I zoned out and continued operating in my rage until I felt like I had peace of mind again. I ran upstairs with the knife in my hand and as I reached the top step's I felt Ray's hand holding my hand with the knife in it.

"What the hell are you doing Ray? Nigga I said let me go for I demolish ya presence!" I was so serious with Ray and couldn't understand why he was tryna keep me from doing what I wanted to do.

"Nah homie, you aint going down like dat, you have too much to live for!"

Ray began tearing up while still trying to take the knife out my hand. It was entirely too early in the morning for this, but I didn't care because my feelings has no time on it. I can be chaotic in the morning and at night, it doesn't matter to me. I kicked Ray in his leg as he fell down the stairs, pulling me with him. I blacked out again and it was like time paused for a moment. I was laying on top of Ray as he remained still. I couldn't move myself for a second.

"Nigga get off of me yo!" Ray said as he tried pushing me off of him.

I stumbled over on the floor remaining still, wondering why I couldn't get up from the ground.

"Oh hell no cuz!"

Ray looked at me with fear in his eyes. I looked back at him and noticed him running into the kitchen and grabbing the phone off the hook. I took a deep breath, feeling numb and as I looked down, I discovered the knife in my shoulder.

"Aye yo, I need an ambulance immediately!"

Ray began panicking over the phone, cursing the operator out. They must have told him to hold for a moment because he remained silent for a couple of seconds.

"Aunt Jackie aint gonna believe this!" Ray said while wrapping the wash towel around the bladed part of the knife that struck my shoulder.

Chapter Twenty One

Life is not the same; it has a meaning when you call its name. I was starting to become devastated, confused, angry, delusional, scarred, scared, overwhelmed, bitter, transformed, violent, disrespectful, miserable, depressed, sick and dreadful within a matter of minutes. I no longer knew what to think, nor did I feel the need to explain anything. It was like my world had been taken away from me and I didn't know how to get it back. To have life, the emotions would correspond with the pulse, guaranteeing that the blood line flows properly. I looked on the front steps as Ray paced back and forth, smoking a cigarette. He looked a little devastated himself as he pounded his head into his hands.

"Get out of the window, boy!" Aunt Jackie said as she stood over top of me.

It was 12:35 in the afternoon and we were waiting for the ambulance to arrive at the house. The stab wound wasn't really bothering me like I expected it to. Every time I would look down at it, it seemed like the blood stopped gushing out from my shoulder. Aunt Jackie had left work early once she found out what happened. Before she got here, me and Ray tried to put things back together the way they were, but our efforts really didn't do us any justice. Ray nailed pictures in front of the holes and even tried to sew the slashes in the couch, but his skills sucked. I would try to help him, but he wouldn't let me because I was injured.

I knew it would be trouble once I seen Uncle Karl and Cousin Veronica getting out of the car in front of the house. I looked back out the window, noticing Ray walking over to Lil Rodney's house to see if he was there I guess. I hate getting involved with the law because I dont like police too much. Although they tell you that they were for you, I felt like they had hidden motives themselves. In the same breath, I knew that Aunt Jackie wasn't going to let this slide under the carpet either, especially if Cousin Veronica and Uncle Karl were here edging her on. I remained speechless as I sat in the reality of things, trying to take everything in at a time.

Aunt Jackie glanced at the door, contemplating if she would be the one to open it. I hope that she didn't expect me to be the one because if I opened it, I would crack that ole man and spit in my cousin's face, forming *imagine me* with my spit. I no longer had a support system or people to call my family.

"Hey, what are ya'll still doing here?" Cousin Veronica came in the door entirely dramatic and loud with a sympathetic look.

Aunt Jackie put a towel over top of the wound so it wouldn't be noticeable or freak anyone out when they seen it.

"They're on their way now." Aunt Jackie said as she grabbed her purse.

Uncle Karl came in a little after Cousin Veronica came in. You know how it takes older people a little more time to get to the front door. When he got in, he didn't speak or even say a word to me. He remained calm and just looked at me with a still look on his face.

"Well can somebody tell me what happened?" Cousin Veronica asked as she pulled out her phone to check for missed calls or new text messages.

"Pretty much his cousin Ray had been staying here with us and I guess this morning they must have gotten into it." Aunt Jackie said as she pulled the stitches out from the couch and took the pictures off the walls, revealing the mess. I hated when Aunt Jackie twisted up my words and told somebody the story, like she was right.

"No No No NO NO NO NO NO NO NO NO that aint right Aunt Jackie!" I said shutting off their conversation before they went any further.

"Everything was cool this morning, but I don't know what happened from the time Uncle Karl called to the time of you calling me about Ray. Now I can admit, I put the holes in the walls and cut the couches up, but it served it purpose!" I was steaming up on the inside again.

"Served its purpose?" Cousin Veronica and Uncle Karl said to themselves at the same time.

"Nephew, you don't have to lie and protect your cousin from the stuff that he's about to get himself into!" I couldn't believe Aunt Jackie still wanted to blame Ray for the destruction.

"He's a grown ass man and could have easily avoided all of this by not staying here! What does Marvin have to say about all of this?" Uncle Karl yelled back as he agreed with Aunt Jackie.

Aunt Jackie apparently didn't tell Mr. Marvin what happened because when Cousin Veronica and Uncle Karl asked, she answered the question indirectly. The ambulance pulled up outside with the siren lights on. The paramedics got out of the truck expeditiously. Soon as we noticed them getting out of the car, Aunt Jackie instantly tried to stand me up and bring me out to them, almost forgetting that Uncle Karl and Cousin Veronica was there.

The paramedic's started knocking on the door as Aunt Jackie went to open it.

"Hello, is the victim able to walk from the home to the back of the truck?" The tall and slinky looking dude said while looking around the house.

"Yes, he's able to get to the truck independently." Aunt Jackie said while putting her purse straps on her shoulder.

"The police will be meeting us at the hospital, correct", I didn't know what Aunt Jackie had planned, but I knew that I didn't like whatever it was already.

"Yes, you wanted to file a report for the victim?" The ambulance man said as he started coming over to me.

"Yes she does, yes that's correct." Uncle Karl said as he cut the guy off from talking. They were taking this a little over board, calling me a victim and getting the police involved like I had been shot or something. I felt nausea as I stood to my feet, thinking about the risk I put Ray into. Aunt Jackie or none of the others didn't believe me when I told them that I did it all. They continuously would blame Ray and say that I was covering up for him and that would make me mad even more.

"Veronica, you and Uncle Karl gonna stay here and try fixing up the house before Marvin gets home." Aunt Jackie said while giving Uncle Karl a kiss on the cheek.

They seemed cool with it and waved us off so that they could get started with the renovations in the house. I never been in the back of an ambulance truck before and it scared me. They had a stretcher for me to lay on and even had numerous amounts of tubes and other first aid stuff on the shelves of the truck. The paramedic's assistant sat in the back of the truck with us so that she could talk to Aunt Jackie. Before the ambulance got to the house, Aunt Jackie told me not to say a word. She insisted that she would tell what happened because she didn't want me saying anything that would have them questioning my residence. I wanted to jab my fingers in her eye balls and tell her that she didn't even know everything that happened.

It was 2:15 pm when we pulled off from my house to go to the hospital. The ambulance lady was talking Aunt Jackie's head off just to see how we lived and how I was raised.

"I'm his guardian and I am always looking after him, that's why it devastates me to allow this type of thing to slip past my eyes." Aunt Jackie was being dramatic as usual.

I really wanted to expose Aunt Jackie and tell the lady that she really didn't know what happened, but because I never was in this type of situation before, I took Aunt Jackie's advice from the house.

"He's a good boy, gets excellent grades in school and oh yeah not to mention, he's graduating high school tomorrow so we got to get this wound closed up", Aunt Jackie looked at me and smiled as she looked back to the lady.

We pulled up to the emergency entrance fast. As the truck came to a complete stop, the lady opened the door so that me and Aunt Jackie could get out of the ambulance. Aunt Jackie really treated me like I was crippled and helpless as we got to the double doors of the hospital, putting on a show. I was surprised when I seen Ray and Lil Rodney pulling up in the parking lot. I knew Ray wouldn't allow any lies to continue because of the great risk that I and now Aunt Jackie was putting him in. Soon as we got inside, the ambulance people took us straight to the exam room so that I could be seen by a doctor.

"Now what are these fools doing here?" Aunt Jackie looked shocked as Ray and Lil Rodney entered into the hospital. I don't think that they saw us when we went to the back because I could see them looking around as I looked through the window of the door we walked through.

"Are you alright nephew?" I couldn't understand why Aunt Jackie was asking me if I was alright. I shrugged my shoulders and continued walking to the room they were putting us in. My phone started vibrating and I seen that it was Lil Rodney calling me.

"Aye man, where you go", Lil Rodney asked as I noticed Aunt Jackie looking at my every move, trying to figure out who it was that I was talking to.

"I'm in the back man; hopefully they don't take long with this. Tell Ray that everything is gonna be aight, I'll be fine…" Aunt Jackie snatched the phone from my hands as she put it to her ear.

"Lil Rodney, you need to go back home and don't have Ray getting you involved in this. You have things going on with you and your family already as it is and you don't need any additional things to be worrying about!" Aunt Jackie said while looking down at my formed fists.

"And what the hell are you gonna do with those fists?" She said while pausing her conversation with Lil Rodney.

I was starting to feel the pain of the stab wound and Aunt Jackie wasn't making anything any better for me. It took everything in me not to flip out on her and loose my mind in this hospital because I would be locked up if I did.

"Oh, that's more like it; I thought so." Aunt Jackie knew the right buttons to press as I got closer to the thin line of beating the crap outta her. She hung up the phone and gave it back to me, looking disturbed.

"I can't believe you RJ, you are becoming exactly what your father was; very disrespectful, selfish and self-centered. This is a serious matter that you shouldn't handle lightly and you are definitely treating it as if it's not serious to you…"

I continued letting her talk and could care less if she came to my graduation. While she still continued to talked, we noticed the police waling into the room.

"Hello, are you Jackie Jones?" The police officer asked while his walky-talky made distorted noises of other officers talking.

"Yes, but Jones is my maiden name." Aunt Jackie said as she glanced at me with a weird looking look on her face.

"Ok and you must be Raven Hill." The officer said to me while pulling out his notepad and looking at my covered up shoulder.

"Yeah, that's me." I didn't know how to respond because I started to choke up for no reason. The officer could tell that I was a little nervous as well, that's why he insisted that I must have been a victim who was stabbed.

"Well what happened to you Mr. Hill?" The officer said to me while looking me directly in the eyes.

"Well… I don't remember everything that happened in

order..." I said as Aunt Jackie sat in her chair, shaking her legs.

"Well I remember everything that happened." Aunt Jackie said cutting me off. She continued talking to the officer as if she was there during the time of the accident and actually blamed it on Ray. She went on and on about how he repeatedly hit me and stabbed me in the shoulder as the officer ordered me to remove the towel so that he could see the wound. "And as a matter of fact, the offender decided to show up and follow us to the hospital!"

I couldn't believe Aunt Jackie was giving in full detail lies about Ray and falsely accusing him as if she didn't know him. I looked at the police officer as he continued writing in his notepad, then seconds later pulling out his handcuffs from his waist.

"Ok, now Mr. Hill is this all true?" The officer asked while reporting everything in his walky-talky. I looked to Aunt Jackie and seen the squinting in her eyes. I felt like I was about to loose breath and fall out right in front of them. I didn't know what would happen if I disagreed to Aunt Jackie's plea to the police officer. "Yes sir".

Chapter Twenty Two

May 29, 2008

    For hours and hours into the new day, I wasn't feeling like myself. I mean yeah, its all apart of human nature, but I'm talking about the kind of feeling that I couldn't shake. I already knew this was becoming a busy and stressful day for me. I had to put all personal feelings aside and focus on what was about to take place later on today, according to Aunt Jackie. With the thought of Ray being arrested, it blew me to know that I had something to do with it. Aunt Jackie was at work, constantly checking on me every other hour. The more I told her that I was fine, the more she seemed to call. Aunt Jackie gave me $30.00 to get a haircut and get something to eat once I was done.

    It was 9:02 am and I really didn't feel like getting up from the bed, but I know what I had to do. My mind wouldn't allow me to forget all that happened yesterday either, from the house to the hospital. Mr. Marvin knew what happened before he even stepped inside last night. Lil Rodney and Ray called his cell phone, warning him of what he was going to face once he got home. I could tell last night that he was feeling some type of way because he went straight up the steps and didn't even eat the dinner that Aunt Jackie prepared for him. I guess he was mad that Aunt Jackie didn't tell him what occurred at the house. She still would walk around the house like nothing ever happened, thinking that he wouldn't notice. I got out of the bed, feeling a little dizzy and woozy. I could tell that I wasn't the same person that I was a few days ago and it started scaring, even me. On my way to the bathroom, I could hear voices calling my name and telling me that my life was in danger. I couldn't control what I was hearing unless I screamed from the top of my lungs. I stood over the sink, looking into the mirror at myself. A dark and horrific voice spoke through the mirror to me.

'RJ what's wrong with you boy, will you ever get enough of me? I guess not son because apparently you're too wrapped up in my identity. You have the image, you have the look and must I add, the attitude. I'm no longer your nightmare because we've established a covenant together, which make things a lot smoother. Less fighting, less bribing; man this is oh so easy. You have given your soul freely to me and for that, I commend you. Now you are safer and I'm serious, safer than you've ever been before. I'm sticking with you forever and ever until your days are no more. That's what you want right? Someone who will support, love and give you the emotional attention that you need? Trust me RJ, I got you son; I'm warning you though, that whatever you do, just don't offend me.'

For the second time in my life, I smiled. I smiled because I knew that I wasn't alone in this and that things were going to be alright with me. On the other side of things, I knew it was Satan who was talking to me and feeding my ego, but I knew that things weren't gonna get any worse than hearing his voice. Funny thing is that as I looked in the mirror real closely, I could see a cloudy image of Aunt Jackie and my dad talking in that deep voice that spoke out to me. As I prepared for my shower, the voices got more and more intense and I even started to see things. Brandon was in the shower with me like how we used to take showers together as little kids.

'Let me get some water so that I can wash this soap off RJ.' Brandon said while shoving me to get to the front of the water sprout. Trying to shake those thoughts, I stood in the shower and let the water pour onto one side of my body as I began to cry.

I couldn't understand what was happening to me and I started to blame Aunt Jackie and Mr. Marvin for this. It would be nights that I felt them laying hands on me while I was sleeping and they would pour oil on me. Then by the time I woke up, I would feel good and as the day went by, I would develop sharp pains in my body. I never told anyone because I didn't want to feed into the pains that I would feel. Aunt Jackie used to say that if I entertained pain that I had no control over, I claimed sickness. I'm telling you, Aunt Jackie had me shook in my younger years and I can laugh about it now though. I got out the shower and then went to my room to get dressed. I looked at the clock that was sitting on the top of my TV and seen that it was 10:50 am already. I started to rush because I scheduled an appointment with my barber at 11:10

and I was twenty minutes away from the barbershop. Slipping on my clothes and shoes, I was out of the house in no time.

I opened the door as I headed out to leave as the sun invaded the house. The weather was just how I liked it, nice and warm with a bright blue sky to look at. The trees were starting to blossom into great art and the flowers started to root from the ground. I was pleased, shaking my head with amazement as I got into my car.

"You're the only one I need in my life; you're the only one I need in my life..." I sang the lyrics to the song playing on the radio.

My phone started ringing nonstop as I looked to see who was calling me.

"Hello." I said while turning down the music.

"Hey nephew, are you alright?" It was Aunt Jackie checking on me again for the hundredth time. My response never changed, just the tone of my voice did.

"Auntie, I told you that I have been fine for hours now and it's gotten to the point of you getting on my nerves." I said as I noticed her chuckling.

"Nephew I know, I know just bare with me because I'm concerned about you." Aunt Jackie was just being a little dramatic I think. "I was also calling to tell you that I seen Tim and his little friend near my job a few minutes ago and was shocked to see his tattoo of her name on his neck. I mean, is it that serious nephew, I'm talking about their relationship", Aunt Jackie went on and on.

"I guess so auntie, they're in love and its nothing anybody can do about it." I said while pulling up at the barbershop. Aunt Jackie laughed as we got off the phone and said that she would call me once she picked Jaime up and got home.

As I walked into the shop, I had seen that it was only two people before me, waiting their turns. I sat in the chair, looking at the Big Booty Judy's special edition magazine. You know how it is in the shop; one of the men would say that reading was fundamental, then would laugh. Graduation was at 2:00 pm and Aunt Jackie was about to get off soon. I was becoming frustrated that Ray wouldn't be able to attend the graduation because that's all he was talking about. He told me and Lil Rodney that he would have posters and signs with our pictures on them and wear a shirt that said, *Only the scholars survive... We all we got... Congrats*. Now, I wonder how me and Lil Rodney's relationship will be without Ray being around. I didn't know if Aunt Jackie would treat him the same or even allow him to come around again.

It was 11:36 am and I was now on my way back to the crib to get my cap and gown ready so that I could head to the auditorium. I wanted to be ready once the time came for me to meet with my classmates for the line up. Aunt Jackie took my gown to the cleaners so that they could press it and have it looking fresh when I put it on. I couldn't believe it; I was graduating and starting to become a man. The real world was approaching me more and more as the minutes passed by. I was so excited about making the next step and becoming a graduate of Downtown high school. Mr. Marvin and Aunt Jackie texted me, counting down the minutes for graduation to start and that gave me a little boost of excitement. I still wished that me and Tim handled our differences before all of this took place though because I knew that things would be weird when we seen each other at graduation. Times that I would want to confront him, I would just let everything go because I had my mind made up that he would call to fix everything and apologize for the way he'd been acting towards me.

"Think positive. Think positive." I told myself while walking up to the front door. I didn't need any other feelings taking control of my current mood.

"Hey nephew, you look sharp baby." Aunt Jackie said while taking a picture as I walked in the front door. "Marvin is on his way with Patrick and the rest of the crew."

Aunt Jackie's mouth was moving 50 miles per hour. I guess she was too excited about today and I didn't blame her. I could also tell that she was holding back her emotions somewhat because of the incident that occurred with Ray yesterday at the hospital. I wanted to make her feel bad without her noticing what my motives were though.

"So how is your shoulder?" She said smiling at me as if everything was alright.

My conscious hit me again and I could feel anger taking over my body. Every time Aunt Jackie brought up yesterday's happenings some kind of way, it would frustrate me for the simple fact that she did more damage than mending the situation. She thought she gave me the satisfaction of being stress free by separating my only relative on my dad's side from me. I didn't think that it was fair and wanted her to feel the pain that I was starting to feel. I sat on the couch quietly grinning as she went into the kitchen to wash the remaining dishes that were left in the sink from last night.

'RJ, you are becoming what I knew you would be. Make me proud even more son, live my dream and enhance your reality.' The dark voice loudly attacked my brain again. I jumped up, being a little caught off guard by the voice because there was no warning.

"RJ what I tell you about leaving your shoes down stairs, I'm telling you; my patience is running thin with you boy!" Aunt Jackie said while walking into the living room area.

I couldn't stand when Aunt Jackie blamed me for Mr. Marvin mistakes and then once I told her that it wasn't me, she would still give me the run around about how she raised a responsible man. I went into the dining area to pick up the shoes, not saying a word to Aunt Jackie as she stood, waiting for me to get them. As I bent down to reach for them, she shoved my head with her hand with force.

"Next time, you come quicker when I tell you to do something. Now go upstairs and get ready to head to the school."

I was through after she put her hands on me. My teeth locked into my jaws and my fists started to form into power balls. I stomped up the stairs with anger and rage in each step that I took. I threw Mr. Marvin shoes in their room, noticing Jaime sleep on the bed.

"I know you ain't throwing stuff!" Aunt Jackie yelled from down stairs.

I didn't reply, but rather smiled as I looked at Jaime breathing in and out. I looked at Aunt Jackie's dresser, noticing an icy hot tube and peroxide sitting next to her bible. Before making another move towards her dresser, I pulled Jaime pants down and opened her pamper. I reached for the Icy hot tube and peroxide bottle and began opening both of the tops to the bottles. I started to grin as I quietly squeezed the icy hot crème onto the inside of her diaper and poured peroxide on top of the crème, watching the combination of both sizzling.

"Pay backs is something else Jackie!" I said to myself while looking at innocent ole Jaime peacefully sleeping.

"I used to be innocent like you until your mother corrupted me into a monster." I began talking to Jaime as she continued to sleep while putting her pamper back together.

I knew that in a matter of minutes, she would begin crying and I would finally feel the satisfaction that Aunt Jackie wanted me to feel.

Chapter Twenty Three

Graduation was a lot simpler this go around I thought. Unlike junior high's graduation, I didn't really remember everything that happened this year with my high school's graduation. Everything was more settled and less emotional; I really didn't build a close knit relationship with my teachers like I did years before I entered high school. The students really didn't seem too involved with the ceremony anyway and I could tell that they were anticipating all of their individual celebrations once it was over. The faculty staff and my class board took their seats on the stage while the rest of my class sat in the first couple of rows in the front. I remember walking through the aisle and seeing Aunt Jackie, Mr. Marvin and the rest of the crew yelling my name as I passed by them. I really didn't feed into it though because Aunt Jackie had me feeling some type of way after she punched me in the chest when she found out what I did to Jaime. She also took my car away from me, which really made me mad.

I also remember seeing Lil Rodney's dad and grandma with balloons in her hands, looking around to see if they seen him in the line as we walked to our seats. I think his grandma had Alzheimer's disease because she just sat in her seat, playing with the balloons as Lil Rodney's dad looked around for Lil Rodney with his camera in his hand.

Another thing I do remember is Tim walking past me as if I never existed. Our friendship had become a total misunderstanding and some things could have easily been avoided if he was mature enough to come to me. Grant it, I could have come to him as well, but I think that if I took the initiative, it would have been a waste of time. I mean if you look at it from my end, Tim had the issue with me and he kinda allowed his girlfriend, Ira to taint the knitted relationship we had. I still managed to speak to his family though as they seen me standing in the line.

June 4, 2008

"Raven, Raven what are you thinking about?"

My psychologist, Ms. Edna asked as I laid down in the chair. Aunt Jackie signed me up with a young people's association psychologist center around the corner from the house. I had counseling sessions every Monday, Wednesday and Friday at 5:00 in the afternoon. I could hear her telling the people on the phone weeks before, that she started noticing some unfamiliar behaviors that she never seen before coming from me, when in all actuality the reason for me acting out was for the sake of love.

I was ready to get out of this office already. Ms. Edna asked me questions about my childhood and relationships that I had with other people. I really didn't give her too much information because I was skeptical about her telling the state on me and getting me put away in the psych ward or something. You may think its crazy, but people are not trust worthy anymore like they used to be. It's like this; everything that you pour out to somebody else may be a waste of time because no one will understand anyway. I put so much effort into trying to find out about my family's history, but nobody wanted to tell me anything. It really hurts every time I think about it though because I have to figure things out on my own. Aunt Jackie should be guilty for it, my dad should be guilty for it and all the rest of my family should be guilty for leaving stuff out.

"So let's begin this exercise, I want you to yell out your emotions towards the people you've listed on your connection sheet." Ms. Edna had me doing these stupid exercises. "Little Rodney…" Ms. Edna copied notes in her pad as I expressed my emotions.

"Uhh, Cool kid from my block. I would say that our connection is content." I looked at her as she wrote down everything I was saying.

"Ok good, what about Tim?" Ms. Edna looked at me as she repositioned in her chair.

"Our connection is cloudy and depressing. I confided so much in him and was later taken advantage of mysteriously." I could tell that Ms. Edna was getting into this exercise because I noticed her slowly putting her pad down as she focused more on me as I talked. She went down the entire list of everybody that I named on the sheet of paper and I wondered the whole time when would it be over.

"Last but not least, your Aunt Jackie." Ms. Edna pulled her glasses further away from her eyes onto the tip of her nose while moving closer to me.

"Aunt Jackie, Aunt Jackie, Aunt Jackie." I paused and tried thinking before I spoke on Aunt Jackie.

"Ummm, I would say that I'm inspired because there are so many levels that we've reached together and I know that there are many things to be revealed in the future." I smiled as I put my hands in back of my head.

Ms. Edna smiled back, reaching for her note pad. For like 3 minutes, there was a sudden pause in the room and no movement was present. I looked up at the ceiling as Ms. Edna continued writing in her note pad, like an interviewer writing comments at an interview.

"Ok well let me start by saying this..." I knew we had more to cover by the way Ms. Edna started taking to me.

"I did a little project of my own just to see if the feelings you had towards your connections with others, matched how they felt about you and your connection with them." Ms. Edna surprised me and I was anxious to see exactly who she came in contact with.

"Let's start with Aunt Jackie..." Ms. Edna began reading the notes on the paper of each person's testimonial.

'My relationship with RJ is a bit apprehensive because I never know what's going on in his head. You know, since he's been a little boy, I've witnessed him transform into a mature young man, but sometimes I think that he's matured entirely too fast. I need him to be more aware of each connection that he has with others and take a deep breath when he faces conflict. Overall, I would say that I am pretty confident in my connection with my nephew, RJ.'

Ms. Edna didn't even allow me to make any comments after she read the testimonial.

"Now we have Ray! Now I must say that Little Rodney helped me out with this one!" My eyes lit up as I drew closer to the paper to see what was on it before she began reading. Ms. Edna covered the paper up from me and started reading while smiling.

'My connection with my cousin RJ is quite adequate if you ask me. I

have experienced him in a way that caused us to have such a close relationship and I can appreciate it. In the last couple of days before being arrested, RJ expressed to me how much he felt protected with me being around, so I really don't know if things changed since then. I've tried calling him and even Aunt Jackie, but no one answer's'.

Ms. Edna looked at me as I looked back at her confused. I must admit that I was at lost for words and really didn't know if I had enough energy to continue listening to all these testimonials. Before she could go any further, I could see a dark shadow walking towards the room from the hall way. Ms. Edna wasn't paying attention because she just kept running her mouth with all of these testimonials. As the shadow got closer, an image appeared when the office light hit it.

"Umm excuse me, but are you guys finished?" Aunt Jackie asked while knocking on the opened office door. Me and Ms. Edna both looked towards the direction of the door to see Aunt Jackie standing at the door with Lil Rodney beside her.

"Ah yes, we were just about finished and were wrapping things up." Ms. Edna said with a smile as she quickly put her folder on the desk.

I didn't understand why Lil Rodney was with Aunt Jackie, especially when he had the responsibility of tending to his grandmother and helping his dad out with her. I sat up in the chair and zoned out, thinking about the major changes that took place in my life. Ms. Edna was telling Aunt Jackie about my progress and what we established today in my counseling session. I really didn't pay Lil Rodney any mind, but I knew that he was too quiet for his own good though.

"Ok, so they will be the plans for next week and the following week."

Ms. Edna showed Aunt Jackie the lesson plans that she created for our counseling sessions. Aunt Jackie shook her head, looking a little uninterested and ready to go. I got up and walked over to Lil Rodney so that I could speak to him as we both waited for Aunt Jackie to finish talking to Ms. Edna.

"Lil Rodney, what's good kid?", I said while dapping it up with him.

"I wish my life was." Lil Rodney looked down while talking as if he had seen a mouse running across the room in his peripheral.

I knew that something had to be up by the way Aunt Jackie

was rushing to leave and the lack of energy Lil Rodney showed. My eyes slowly followed his eyes to the direction of the floor and on the journey down, I seen a series of welts on his arms and a great black streak across his neck.

"Come on yall." Aunt Jackie said as she got a head start in the halls.

"Yo lil Rodney, what happened to you nigga?" I started to think about the Hudson boys and how they served Lil Rodney back in the day.

"RJ don't worry about it, see there you go minding other people's business. What will it take for you to learn that you are an intriguing little bastard?" Aunt Jackie yelled at me the entire way to the car while Lil Rodney kept his head down. At the same time, I couldn't believe that Aunt Jackie was over reacting the way that she was, becoming loose mouthed with her words.

"I don't think you want to be calling me an intriguer because last time I checked, you are slowly becoming a manipulator auntie."

My blood levels started to rise and I felt tension as the muscles in every part of my body began to flex. Aunt Jackie stopped everything that she was doing and was about to throw a blow to my face it looked like, but she was stopped by Lil Rodney.

"Yo on a real, take me back to the crib, I'll handle my situation on my own." Lil Rodney was frustrated and I could tell that he wanted to explode at any minute.

I was too distracted to even check and see what was going on with him because Aunt Jackie really pissed me off.

"No Lil Rodney, you're not going back to that house. Ya dad made up a reason to pick a fight with you and the sudden death of your grandmother seemed to be it." Aunt Jackie began softening up her voice as she enhanced more of a sympathetic tone.

Lil Rodney began crying while sitting in the back, covering up his face. I knew that the death of Lil Rodney's grandmother had to be a tragedy to his family because although she was sick, she seemed to be the life of their family. I began chuckling to myself as I noticed Aunt Jackie looking at me with rage in her eyes. Usually I'm the type to feel the emotions of other people, but for some strange reason I couldn't develop that mechanism with Lil Rodney's situation. I started to think about the time after graduation when he introduced me to her and she pulled down her pants and pulled off her pamper in front of us and said that she wanted to go skinny dipping.

"Poor old lady", I noticed myself speaking out publicly and tried keeping myself from laughing again. Lil Rodney wasn't paying attention because his emotions overwhelmed him, but I could tell that Aunt Jackie wanted to slice up my guts. She wasn't dumb though because I would be the one to make the first move and chop off her knuckles with a butcher knife, smearing *imagine me* in her blood with my middle finger.

Chapter Twenty Four

As I think about it now, I could tell that Ms. Edna wanted to continue with our session. Aunt Jackie didn't have to come into the office the way that she did, interrupting me and Ms. Edna's quality time. I started to laugh as I stood in the kitchen, drinking some of Mr. Marvin's homemade lemonade tea. Aunt Jackie was in the other room trying to explain Lil Rodney's situation to Mr. Marvin as Lil Rodney sat on the couch quietly. My family know they can assist with other people, but can barely tend to issues within this house. As I walked towards the front room, I could hear Lil Rodney talking to Aunt Jackie and Mr. Marvin.

"I understand what you saying Aunt Jackie, but my dad didn't have to go off on me like that. I mean, really though; it surprised us all, but to blame me for her death ain't right. For real for real, he gave her an early pass to her grave because he really didn't take care of her like he tells everybody in the family. Grandma Roy would always tell me that my dad was mean to her and wouldn't even feed her." Lil Rodney continued talking, getting more and more emotional as he talked.

"I don't mean to be telling all of my family's business, but my dad is a hard core alcoholic and it turns into situations like these. I thought that he would break those habits once he started taking care of Grandma Roy, but I think it made him worse."

I started to think about everything Lil Rodney was saying and it started to open my heart. I knew that Lil Rodney was the type of kid who played the strength in his family, just like me. I listened to him talk about his life as a young buck and how his dad raised him. Because his mom was a strong drug addict, it pushed his dad into having bad anxiety, causing him to be an alcoholic. The only difference between Lil Rodney and I was that he knew the root of his family's history and how situation's in his life happened the way they did. It wasn't that easy for me though because I had to figure out the major pieces of the puzzle on my own and once I discovered something, it was too late. I looked at how involved Aunt Jackie and Mr. Marvin seemed to be in Lil Rodney's problems with his family and it made me feel some type of way. I started mumbling to myself as I walked up the stairs to go to my room. I thought about my life and what mattered to me the most. Tim was no longer in the equation and everybody else was too involved to even consider being apart of my equation. I shut my door, locking it as anger filled my insides. Caring less about the people and what they had to offer me, I fell to the foot of my bed, reaching for my Voodoo dolls that I bought with the money I got from graduating. I created one for Tim, Aunt Jackie, Cousin Veronica, Uncle Karl and even my dad. The owner of the store where I purchased the dolls helped me cast a spell on each doll.

"No...Body knows the trouble you see, huh?"

I said as I pulled out my box of pins that I got with the dolls. The pins were color coated, symbolizing different meanings to each one. I opened the box of pins, laying them out on the cover spread of my bed. Aunt Jackie's doll looked just like her, from the hair to the fake smile she gave people at times. With anxiousness, I quickly stabbed the doll in the stomach area with a pin. I said a quick prayer as I covered my thumb over the pin. I knew that my life was forming into a downward spiral to my grave. It no longer mattered to me because I knew that I would be embraced more once I was there. I smiled at the doll and kissed the pin where I placed it, squeezing the fluffy head. About a half a minute later, a white cat appeared in my room with white eyes.

"Come here kitty kitty, come here girl."

I was overjoyed to get the company of a lost soul to join me. I knew that this cat would give me guidelines and helpful tips to fulfill the needs I was seeking. The little white cat slowly walked over to the side of the bed with her mouth stretched wide open. "Meow, Meow", the cat started to purr as she revealed her freshly sharpened claws. I placed Aunt Jackie's voodoo doll in front of the cat to see what response I would get and before I knew it, the cat took a jab into the head of the doll. I laughed so hard that it was unbelievable, but the interesting thing about it was that once the cat attacked the doll, she turned into a black cat.

"Wooooooooow!" I couldn't believe my eyes and to be honest, I thought it was fascinating. My room door started to vibrate as the cat began hissing with anger.

"RJ, open up this door NOW!" Aunt Jackie yelled as she continuously banged on the door. I quickly threw everything under my bed as I noticed the black cat disappear into the air.

"Auntie, I'm coming."

I tried to kill seconds by talking as I put everything away. I rushed to the door and as I twisted the knob to open it, I noticed that no one was on the other side of the door. I had lost track of time and didn't know where Aunt Jackie or Mr. Marvin went that fast. I shut my bed room door as I ran downstairs, skipping some steps. Aunt Jackie and Mr. Marvin were still talking to Lil Rodney about his problems. I guess it was my conscious that led me to believe Aunt Jackie was knocking on my door. Everyone looked at me as if I was interrupting a very important moment.

The house phone started to ring. As I reached for the phone, Aunt Jackie quickly grabbed it out of my hand. As she answered the call, I noticed that she instantly slammed the phone back onto the hook. She went back to her seat on the couch and with out noticing, I looked on the caller ID to see that it was Ray calling.

"So you just gonna bang on my cousin like that Aunt Jackie?" Smoke escaped through my mouth as the hairs on my arms began to rise.

"Let me tell ya'll something, I thought Ray was someone that I see he's not. He led me and my husband to believe that his motives were pure, when in fact he wanted to set you up with your dad."

Aunt Jackie was blowing me and what made me even madder was that Mr. Marvin agreed to what she was saying.

"RJ, your father has threatened my household with things that he told Ray he wanted to say and do to my wife and myself because we held you from him."

Mr. Marvin placed his hand on my shoulder while talking. I

took in everything that they were saying and smiled. They couldn't figure out exactly why I was smiling, but I knew why I was smiling. I was happy to know that my dad still cared about me and wanted me to still be apart of his life. I scoped the living room area as Lil Rodney, Mr. Marvin and Aunt Jackie remained silent while looking at me in a weird way. I counted to ten in my mind and then quickly grabbed Mr. Marvin car keys from the table. I didn't hear anyone running behind me as I rushed out of the door, so everything was cool to me. I got in the car and locked the doors, chuckling with the excitement of having a great turn out. As I pulled out of the driveway, I saw Mr. Marvin and Aunt Jackie running out of the door, trying to catch me. It was too late by then because I was out in the wind. I blasted the music, hitting up to 90 miles per hour onto the highway.

"Timmy boy, hope you ready for what I'm about to give you, my nigga!"

Rage grew more and more into the pores of my body as I thought about everything Tim put me through. Aunt Jackie and Mr. Marvin probably thought I acted out because of what they were telling me about my dad, but I could care less about that because I seen Tim's name repeatedly on the caller ID. I wondered what was going on with that and if he was keeping in touch with Aunt Jackie or even Mr. Marvin. My phone continuously rung, but I ignored it every time. I guess Aunt Jackie threatened to call the police on me according to her text message to me.

"I ain't scared of those Pigs, hoe!"

I started laughing while getting off the exit to Tim's house. It was 9:35 pm when I pulled up at Tim's front door with a blade under my sleeve. I stole this blade from Uncle Karl's house the day me and Aunt Jackie helped clean his house. The lights were out in Tim's house, but I could see his bed room light on. Being the type of raged person I am, I decided to climb up the ledge of Tim's house. I made sure that nobody was around to see me climbing up the wall. As I reached the top of the roof, I instantly pulled out an orange face mask that I got from Mr. Marvin's closet and covered my face with it.

"No…body knows the trouble I see, No…Body knows but me" I started singing the tunes to Aunt Jackie's song and started chuckling as I thought about her singing it.

I got on my knees, crawling to Tim's bedroom window and

knocked on it. I didn't even check to see if Tim was in there, but it was too late to turn around now. As I placed my back against the wall of the house, I could see the shadow of Tim looking out of the window.

"This nigga scared!" I started laughing as I heard the noise from Tim's window opening up.

Without thinking, I pulled out the blade from the inside of my sleeve and stood to my feet. As I turned to the direction of the window, me and Tim locked eyes.

"I never expected for things to happen this way nigga. You was never my homie to start with." Tim started to panic as he remained blank-faced.

"Yo, you tripping RJ and this is exactly what I'm talking about!" Tim began pleading his case as to why he was treating me the way he was. It seemed that during the length of him talking to me, I got angrier.

"Well all imma say is... *Imagine me* nigga!"

I curled the blade into his neck as blood gushed from his mouth instantly. I jumped from the roof, noticing Tim screaming for help as he held his blood-filled neck. I made it to the car within seconds and pulled off as I noticed the lights coming on in the house. I wasn't worried at all because I had nothing to loose. Everything was going great for me and just to celebrate, I took a trip to Seven Eleven before going back to the crib. It was 10:23 pm as I pulled back into the drive way of my town house. The front door was open and as I walked up to open the screen door, I seen Aunt Jackie crying on the couch while holding Jaime.

"RJ do you know what you just did?" Aunt Jackie screamed as she shoved Jaime onto Mr. Marvin.

"Auntie, chill...Chill!" I said while slurping on my slurpee. "I only went to the store and now I'm back, see." I smiled as I noticed Mr. Marvin looking at me with disgust in his eyes.

Chapter Twenty Five

June 13, 2008

As the days of each week passed, my emotions and behavioral habits began getting more crucial than they ever were before. I felt like I was too drained to explain myself to anybody and I knew that if I explained myself, no one would understand how I was feeling. Nothing was the same to me anymore and I could tell that Aunt Jackie and everybody else were catching on to the changes taking place in my life. I felt that my moods were good moods though because I was more aware of my feelings and alert of things that I allowed to slip once before. My counseling sessions with Ms. Edna didn't make things any better and the talks with Mr. Marvin were simply in vein. I laughed at everybody who attempted to talk to me about my own personal problems, like I would easily spill the beans to them. Mr. Marvin was preparing for his men's conference, so that left me and Aunt Jackie here with Jaime.

For the last couple of days, I started isolating myself from everybody. Word hit the streets a little late about Tim's death, although his funeral just passed this Tuesday at some Pentecostal church on Lumbard Ave. Tim's mom, Ms. Brenda was so glad to see me, Aunt Jackie and Mr. Marvin walking into his funeral that day. I didn't feel any guilt and really didn't want to be there, but Aunt Jackie forced me to go. Some dude named Prince was apparently arrested for Tim's death because it was investigated that Prince was the last person seen with Tim and that he was planning to set Tim up for what he did to Prince's cousin, Ira. I knew that Ira was no good, but I was also glad that they threw everything on Prince before they even thought about tracking our history. I knew how to cover up my tracks, being very wise of how things were done. I put Uncle Karl second on my hit list once I handled things with Tim first.

Things were comfortable at this point and it was no way that I would get caught up if I played my cards right. I knew that this weekend was gonna be a boring one because Mr. Marvin was going away. I could tell that he was starting to second guess about going since so much stuff was going on around here. Mr. Marvin brought his bags to the front of the door as he ran into the kitchen to grab a bottled water from the refrigerator.

"Babe, hurry up! Your plane comes in an hour and I know that the other men are waiting for you."

As much as Aunt Jackie didn't want him to go, she started rushing the time for him to leave the house. She had to drop him off at the airport since he was leaving his car behind. I was hype because Mr. Marvin was letting me hold his car until he got back from his trip with the men. I sat on the couch, planning my weekend out and how things were gonna go for me. I knew that on Sunday, church would be dry because Pastor Clay was going on the trip as well and one of those low budget preachers would have to take over.

"Nephew, be cool man and take care of the family while I'm away." Mr. Marvin said to me as he patted me on my shoulder before heading out.

"I got you Unc." I started smiling as the door shut behind him and Aunt Jackie. I knew that it was about to go down this weekend and that I was unstoppable.

Tonight I wanted to go out with Gina because we never shared any intimate time alone. I mean, we would talk on the phone every day, but I really didn't grasp the full effect of who she was since I never experienced chillin' with her in person.

"Yeah boy, how you gon' act!" I jumped up from the couch and rushed up stairs so that I could get dressed.

It was 10:31 am and I wanted to start my day early today because I had a lot to do before the night hit. Lil Rodney asked Aunt Jackie if he could stay with us for the weekend to keep us company and she agreed to it. While getting my clothes out before hitting the shower, I made a quick call to Gina, just so that I could reserve my space with her.

"Hello. Hey daddy!" Gina started calling me daddy and that let me know that I was in there!

"Sup babe, yo let's go out tonight. I'm thinking, Damond

Gray's Comedy Lounge." I crossed my fingers, being a little sucker for love, hoping that she had no other plans for tonight.

"I'm wit' it if you wit' it daddy."

I was hype that our date was set and that I had something to look forward to. I had a lot on my mind and just wanted to have some fun to take everything away. We ended our conversation with a verbal kiss and a few see you laters.

Let's fast forward a little bit, so I got dressed and made it out of the house just in time to get some breakfast from Joe Buck's Deli on 15th and Franklin. When I pulled up to the place, I could see a pool of old men sitting up on the stools, eating their breakfast. It grossed me out to see older people eating food, from the looks of their loose dentures stuffed with a combination of food particles and slobber, to the miserable looks on their faces. I passed up breakfast and decided to go pass my mom's grave site instead before going on with the rest of my day. I was a little skeptical about going to see her because of what I went through the last time I went. Her grave site was three blocks away from Joe Buck's Deli, so it wasn't out of the way.

It was now 11:23 am and Aunt Jackie sent a text to check on me while she was at work. I pulled up to the grave yard, clinching my hands to the stirring wheel. Every time I came to visit my mom's grave site, I always would feel nausea and didn't know why. The sun was beaming and the sky was clear as the day filled with color. I guess that going to a grave site this early was a little weird because nobody was out. I tried walking around other people's stones because it gave me the creeps when I walked over them. As I walked up to my mom's grave stone, I noticed something different that freaked me out more than the letter I seen the last time. My mother's grave site was dug up more than a little over two feet with a shovel standing beside it. I looked around to see if anybody was in walking distance that could have possibly done this, but I didn't see a soul. I was on my way to the memorial's office in the front to report this occurrence, but I stopped my tracks once I seen a man walking into the grave yard with a black leather trench coat on and a hood, with a large stick in his hand. I didn't bother to move or run because I couldn't feel my legs and I had no urge to react to him. As he took off the hood from his head, I noticed that it was a man who traumatized my insides every time I expected it to be him, and this time it was.

My mind joined soul ties with gas as it escaped through my rear end. It was my dad and I knew that he knew it was me because he started yelling out my name as he locked eyes with me. I ran as fast as I could into the dugout hole and tried covering it back up with the dirt that stood on the side. "I wanna die, I wanna die," was all that I kept repeating to my self as I laid under the dirt, noticing the rhythm of my heart slowing down. I could hear his voice getting closer as I slowly tried pulling out the blade from my pocket.

"What are you doing? What are you DOING KID?" I heard my dad screaming as the light from the sky started to open my dark place of safety underground.

"Dad, just leave me alone!" I yelled as I started throwing blows at him realizing that it was a grave yard worker.

"What are you doing kid? Get out of here before I call the police!"

I jumped up from the hole, covered with dirt and grass; rushing to jump in the car. I wanted to call Aunt Jackie to tell her what they did to my mom's grave site, but she'd probably freak me out even more. At times like these, I wish Ray was around because he knew exactly how to calm me down whenever my thoughts got too carried away. My phone began to ring and as I looked down, I seen that it was Aunt Jackie.

"Auntie you called at the right time because I was just gonna ask if you could set up an appointment for us to go see Ray tomorrow." I was determined to make it happen and I didn't care how Aunt Jackie felt about it.

"Oh, uhh sure baby", Aunt Jackie said as she snorted. "I wanted to talk to him anyway and get some things straight." Aunt Jackie could never just let things go because she never liked to feel as though she was being played by someone.

I remained silent until she felt best to end the conversation. During the time she was talking, I started to think about Ray more and started to wonder how he was holding up while being locked up. After getting off the phone with Aunt Jackie, I thought that it would be best if I switched my phone's volume to vibrate to show respect at the site. I looked at my watch and seen that it was 12:10 pm. Time was going by fast today and I wasn't complaining at all because I was anticipating my date with my baby, Gina. On the flip side of me being happy and anticipating, I didn't want rage to destroy our time together because I know how things easily get to me, causing a shift in my feelings. The crazy part is that I really can't define my inner man, but I know that he is a mysterious kid with a heart. When being placed in confusion, he would act out and would even scare me at times because this was somebody I was carrying inside of me.

    I pulled up into the driveway of the house, glancing across the street to Lil Rodney's house with my eyes. I wanted to tell Aunt Jackie so bad about the trip to my mom's grave site, but I just decided to wait until she got off from work. *Buzz…Buzz* My cell started vibrating in my left pocket, causing the change at the bottom of my pocket to make noise. As I got to the top step, I noticed Lil Rodney walking behind me.

    "Aye yo, I was just calling you to see where you was at so I could come over." Lil Rodney said while flicking his Black and mild roach. "Pop's going through it and I'm not in the mood for his bull yo."

    Lil Rodney looked like he hadn't been sleep in a week straight and I could tell that he was bothered by the habits of his drunken dad. We walked inside of the house and chilled in the living room, playing a game of Black jacks with Mr. Marvin's new deck of cards.

    "Yoooooo, I'm going out with ole girl tonight and it's going down homie."

    I was hype and couldn't keep the feelings to myself. I wanted things to go smoothly so that I could steal Gina's heart from the other potentials before they even got a chance.

    "Nigga you know I wanna know everything, including how tight it was!"

    Lil Rodney started laughing, but I wasn't because I wasn't thinking what he was thinking. That's the problem with a lot of niggas, they don't know how to control their hormones whenever they around a female and it blows me. If it was another girl, then I would probably consider, but I knew that Gina was a keeper so I didn't want to mess anything up. *Ring…Ring…Ring* the house phone started going off in the middle of our conversation and card game.

    "Yes Auntie." I hate when Aunt Jackie gets too carried away with trying to keep tabs on me.

    "RJ baby, go upstairs in my room and read me Marvin's

account number from the paper on my dresser."

Lil Rodney turned on the TV to the music channel as I went upstairs. As I entered Aunt Jackie's room, I couldn't believe the junk of mess they were keeping in this room. I read her the numbers while looking at myself in the mirror moments after.

"Thanks nephew, now get out of my room and don't be snooping around for nothing." She chuckled as my image in the mirror became still.

"I got you Auntie." I said as I smiled with anticipation while hanging up the phone.

I think that people make things worse when they tell you not to do something because it gives the other person easy access to do the opposite. I began looking through Aunt Jackie and Mr. Marvin's room, hoping that I found something I could blackmail them for later. I couldn't find anything and I began to get frustrated because I knew that if I looked in the right places, I would end up finding something. I looked down at the drawers as I began my search, thinking that I would find porn. I opened the second drawer to the left of the window and noticed a space full of underwear and bras. Aunt Jackie had some explicit sets, I guess for her and Mr. Marvin's pleasure. I began chuckling in amazement of the different styles I seen before I was interrupted by some pictures at the bottom of the underwear. I pulled the pictures out of the drawer and in the pile of pictures; I noticed a loose leaf folded up piece of paper. It was pictures of me and Uncle Karl from when I was a baby and pictures of me with my dad when I was in Kindergarten. I smiled as I thought about the many memories I had with my dad, but didn't really understand the pictures of me and Uncle Karl. As I picked up the folded piece of paper, I shut Aunt Jackie's door so that Lil Rodney didn't interrupt me. My mouth dropped and instantly my heart began beating with anger and rage as my eyes grew smaller. Aunt Jackie had been keeping up with my dad after all and this letter from her to him was proof of it.

Chapter Twenty Six

All day yesterday I stayed to myself, thinking about possible secrets that Aunt Jackie and my dad were holding from me. While reading the letter, the only thing I got out of it was Aunt Jackie pleading to my dad to leave us alone and that she would handle *it* on her own when she felt like *it* was the right time to. I wondered what she meant by *it* and could tell automatically that *it* was something juicy. On top of that, Gina stood me up because she apparently forgot that she made other plans with her friends; that added to the fire. I didn't want to be around nobody, hold conversation with nobody or even look at nobody because I didn't want to victimize the innocent. Lil Rodney ended up not staying because Aunt Jackie didn't want anything to do with his dad tripping out on her. From the time that Aunt Jackie got off of work till now, I have just been in my room by myself.

"Dag Brandon, why you leave me out here by myself nigga?"

I began cursing out what was considered a departed soul and it caused my inner man to slowly rise through my pores. All my life, I've been loosing people left and right, whether it was because of me or out of my control.

It was 9:29 am and Aunt Jackie and I were on our way to go and see Ray at the city's jail downtown. Jaime stayed the night with Ms. Connie, so that left me here by myself with Aunt Jackie.

"RJ come on boy, we're gonna be late for this appointment

you wanted so bad."

Aunt Jackie stood on the other end of the door as I listened to her annoying voice attack the sound waves throughout the house. Without saying a word, I jumped from my bed and opened the door with my fists balled up.

"I got you, what are you yelling for", I said as I started raising my voice; trying to compete with Aunt Jackie's.

"I don't know who in the hell you're talking to, but you have the wrong one young fellow. Get downstairs before I cave ya chest in with my fist!"

Aunt Jackie wasn't making anything better at all because I was three seconds away from jabbing her in the eye with my blade, kicking her down the steps with the *imagine me* print of my shoe on her back. Not saying a word, I grilled her with my teeth clinched together as I stomped down the steps.

"Bastard, do you have anything that you have to say to me?" Aunt Jackie said while shoving me down the steps, fueling my fire even greater than it was before.

"Ahhhhhhhhhh yo stop pushing me, you don't have to put ya hands on me to get ya point across!" I'm telling you, Aunt Jackie better had left me alone or stuff woulda got real quick.

"Bastard, who are you talking to? Huh, who are you talking to RJ?"

Aunt Jackie continued talking just as I put my shoes on so I could get in the car. At this time, it was now 9:38 am and our appointment was at 10:05 am. Aunt Jackie went to the kitchen and came back into the living room with a tea cup in her hand as if we had a lot of down time before our visitation with Ray. *Ding-Ding-Da-Da… Ding-Ding-Da-Da* Aunt Jackie's cell phone started going off as she put her cup on the table.

"Hell, fooling with you I done left my phone upstairs." Aunt Jackie said as she went chasing after it.

"Tramp you should of left me alone, skank!"

I was pissed and felt like being very disrespectful towards the lady I once had the utmost respect for, for years. Before Aunt Jackie came back downstairs, I quickly snorted into her cup as I released mucus from my mouth. I almost succeeded in dropping a pin in the cup too, but I heard her at the top of the stairs coming back down. I stood at the door and waited until she drank from the cup of tea before we headed out.

"I hope you have your I.D with you because your gonna need it."

Aunt Jackie said while taking the last sip of my creative concoction. I smirked as I noticed Aunt Jackie squinting up her face, swallowing the last bit of what was left in the cup.

"I must have put too much honey in my tea."

Aunt Jackie said as I turned to the door to open it. We finally got to the prison a little after our expected time. Aunt Jackie rushed to park because she said that they were very strict when it came to arriving to a visit late.

"I need your I.D please." The officer said as Aunt Jackie signed her name on the role log. As we walked through the metal detector, sweat formed on my finger tips. I hate walking through these things because I always think it will go off on my turn.

"All persons that have a visitation at this time please stand and follow me." The police officer instructed as me and Aunt Jackie walked in his direction along with the other people.

We got to the auditorium as we waited for Ray and the other prisoners to come out to their families.

"You better not be silent during this visitation either because this is what you wanted." Aunt Jackie kept reminding me like she regretted coming to see Ray.

"Now time for visitation." The intercom released its sound throughout the jail as inmates began pouring into the auditorium. I was excited to see Ray because I wanted to catch him up on a lot of stuff that was happening with the family and myself. As we watched all of the other inmates coming out, we were starting to wonder where Ray was at.

"He's probably at the end of the line." Aunt Jackie said as she smiled at me like nothing happened earlier.

I'm telling you, this woman is bi-polar and I swear she is. Ray came from among the other inmates with anger in his eyes and his hands cuffed together connected to the chains on his feet.

"Dag, it's that deep?" I said as Ray sat on the bench across from me and Aunt Jackie.

"Man, yeah and these niggas be trippin' in here yo." Ray began talking to me without acknowledging Aunt Jackie one time.

"Well hello sir, can't you speak?" Aunt Jackie said while cutting off our conversation. Ray looked at her with the nastiest look that I've ever seen before and I knew that it was about to go down.

"Psst, I'm surprised you came to see me! You ain't care about my feelings and you kept ignoring my phone calls. I know Lil Rodney told me."

Aunt Jackie tried talking over him but Ray over powered her.

"For the longest time, I would battle in my brain, giving you the benefit of the doubt. But right now, I'm fully convinced of how you feel about me and what ya' love is all about."

I couldn't believe what was being said and apparently Aunt Jackie couldn't either.

"Excuse me, I think you might wanna' come correct!" Aunt Jackie began getting in her feelings as her legs started shaking.

"Nah… Nah… Nah, I'm not done talking, it's time you hear me out for a change. See, that's the problem with you, it's either ya' way or no way, but I'm bout to switch up the game. To be honest with you, I don't even know why I'm here up in this pin. Guess I was just apart of that generational curse you was talking about, causing me to lose and the system to win." Ray began beating his fists into his lap. "Yeah, Imma' blame it on you and Imma' definitely give you a reason why; because you abused my character and captured my soul with all of your deceitful lies about how you would take care of me and make sure that I'll be the one to fulfill all of my dreams. But nah, it's too late for all dat' though cause I'm long far fetched by ya' misery!"

I knew that Ray hit home with Aunt Jackie because tears started piling up in her eyes as she remained quiet. This was the first time that I seen Aunt Jackie humble herself in a long time and it felt kind of good to witness it, although I wanted Ray to stop.

"Ok, I see where this is going so let me just calm down for just a minute. I'll be deep wit' you and go to the spiritual side of things, than afterwards I'm returning back to the natural side once I'm finished. It's crazy that I gotta' do all of this, just to prove my point on how I feel; church people is amazing. But yet, you were the one who claimed to understand me in the beginning, causing me to now realize that I was cursed by my conduct cause I had too much conversation."

Ray began forming foam on the side of his mouth because he had been talking non stop.

"Normally, the average church person would tell me to pray

about it, take it to God and see what he has to say. Instead, you wanted to know my every move, so now my vision is paralyzed and my eagerness to live right fell astray. I don't even feel right walking inside the church's four walls because like you, so much stuff has changed. I'm hearing that it's competitive like out here and to be honest with you, that's a shame. It's all in who you know now for people to do things for you, when did that ever occur? They don't even know how to keep it casual no more, neglecting GOD, because their desire to bond with other people is much stronger".

I started to feel sorry for Aunt Jackie, but I knew that this was the right thing she needed to better herself. I couldn't be the one to say it because she would have slapped me in my face a long time ago.

"It's a lot to take in, I know; shit gets real. I also know I'm not the only one feeling like this, I don't front because this is simply how I feel. Now Imma wrap this thing up and leave you speechless and hopefully you take heed and see." Ray began standing to his feet as if the guard came to him so that he could return back to his cell. "Trust me, I'll be alright, I'm sane; just know that this weakness in being too transparent to the wolves will be the strength of me. Imma 23 year old male that's reachable to all sinners, I don't judge em' by their issues, but I help transition em' to winners. I'll be the kingdom builder where I'm at, no need to shift my mindset or change my attitude. I have so much power invested in me, no need to talk about it though because I'll let my actions speak for me. I don't need no recognition from none of ya'll cats because it gets old and it's becoming an extinction. I'll be the one to exempt myself from the fakes and live a lifestyle of distinction."

Ray began walking to the back as Aunt Jackie cried even harder. I began laughing inside though because I knew that she felt helpless and cornered into a wall all at the same time.

"Come on RJ, let's go." Aunt Jackie said as she stood to her feet so that the guard could let us leave our visitation early.

We got in the car and things got really quiet. It was just how I liked it and I started feeling good again, like my old self. I still wanted some answers from Aunt Jackie though, but I decided that I was going to wait once she came off of her high emotional mountain.

"So the grave yard workers apparently dug up the wrong tombstone, which was your mother's and now they owe us big time." Aunt Jackie started to calm down a little, still seeming very tense.

"I knew that it was a mistake." I said as we got off of the exit to go back home. The funny thing is, the entire time we were driving back home, Aunt Jackie never mentioned what it was that Ray was saying, as if he was speaking truth about everything that he was saying.

"No... Body knows the trouble I see, nobody knows but me!!" Aunt Jackie began singing her infamous song again as I noticed her shaking non stop. *"Nobody knows, but me… Nobody knows, but me!"* she began repeating the last bars to the song as I noticed an increase in speed with the car.

Before I could open my mouth to utter a word out, we rammed into a silver colored parked Saturn car. For a moment, I couldn't open up my eyes because my body felt numb, even my eye lids. I could hear people outside, screaming and surrounding the entrance of our neighborhood.

"Aunt Jackie, are you cool?" I asked while waiting for a response. I slowly opened up my eyes and noticed Aunt Jackie's head turned to the direction of the driver's window, not moving.

Chapter Twenty Seven

Mr. Marvin decided to call his arrival back in town a little early because of our car accident. Aunt Jackie was not conscious during the time she ran into the car and I don't think she even realized everything that was happening after it was all said and done. (I know that you're probably saying that something is wrong with me, but I promise you that my Aunt Jackie is worse off than I am.) Mr. Marvin came into the house with disappointment and fear in his eyes. I don't really think that he knew everything because he would constantly ask me questions. Aunt Jackie had to stay in the hospital because she fractured her hip and her jaw. I'm surprised that she didn't break her neck because it looked like she was able to turn it all the way around like in the exorcist, how that girl in the movie turned her neck in a 360 degree circular motion.

Ha! Enough with the jokes, I had been home chilling after I got checked out at the hospital. I really don't know what happened with Aunt Jackie and what caused her to go in such a depressing state, running into a car. She didn't want me worrying, so she told me to go back home and give Mr. Marvin a call, telling him what happened to us. I'm not even gonna lie though, I called Mr. Marvin and two hours later, he was back home.

"Nephew, what happened and I want to know everything." Mr. Marvin said as he grabbed the phone, I guess so that he could call Aunt Jackie. I began explaining the situation to him about our travel home after the visit we had with Ray.

"Oh how is Ray?" Mr. Marvin asked, noticing blood tracks dripping on the floor.

"Oh, he's doing good, he seemed to be in a good mood." I said as my eyes followed his eyes.

My forehead started collecting sweat drops and my motives

began increasing as anger traveled through my brain. Mr. Marvin seen that my hands were in back of me as I was sitting on the couch and began walking closer to me as he followed the tracks.

"Nephew, let me see your hands, where is this blood coming from?" Mr. Marvin asked as he reached for my hidden hands.

Within seconds, I revealed my hands, throwing the Voodoo dolls that I created of him and Aunt Jackie and started laughing. After my prayer while I was alone, I noticed the dolls bleeding red blood and it made me realize how real this stuff was and I guess Mr. Marvin was surprised with it all because his facial expression exposed his thoughts. I started laughing as he looked at the Voodoo dolls layng on the ground.

"What in the hell is going on with you man?" Mr. Marvin looked at me as if he wanted to hit me.

Before I knew it, I seen the black cat again and it seemed mad. White rats with red eyes started coming from the cat's mouth, as if it was throwing its food back up. I smiled as I picked up one of the white rats while it ran to Mr. Marvin's Voodoo doll. Mr. Marvin didn't know what I was doing, but I'm telling you, my eyes weren't playing tricks on me. I opened my mouth as I held the rat by the tail, watching it dangling over my mouth. As I released it in my mouth, I felt it running through my body, tearing up my insides.

"Don't do too much damage little guy." I started chuckling as Mr. Marvin continued looking at me in amazement, as if I was hallucinating. The phone began ringing throughout the house as Mr. Marvin ran after it while keeping his eyes on me.

"What's wrong Mr. Marvin?" I felt a little tipsy and groovy all at the same time as I stood to my feet.

"Uh hello, Imma call you back." Mr. Marvin hung up the phone and charged at me, just as I dropped to the floor, crawling on my knees to the basement of the house. In my mind, I felt like I was in a movie running from a killer or something. I turned my head just to see if he was following me and to my surprise he was. I started laughing even more as I did a u-turn back up the stairs to the couch.

"RJ, what is going on with you boy?" Mr. Marvin was not feeling this and I could tell that he wanted to do something about it.

" No... Body knows the trouble I see, nobody knows but me!" I tried reenacting the scene from the time of the accident but it didn't work out. Mr. Marvin grabbed me by my waist and picked me up as he carried me to the car.

It was 3:12 in the afternoon and it felt like 6:30 at night. I started feeling normal again and was wondering why I was still in this room, waiting on somebody to come and see me. I was supposed to go out on my rescheduled date with Gina, but I don't think it's gonna happen because Mr. Marvin had me at this hospital getting checked out by the doctors again for the second time. After drawing blood from me and even taking the initiative to give me a CAT scan, they told Mr. Marvin that I was already in the third stage of the rapid eye movement behavior disorder, which was basically stating that I was responding and acting out on my dreams. They said it would only get worse if it wasn't treated, but other than that nothing was wrong with me and I was completely healthy. He continued asking questions and didn't seem ok about it, but respected their judgment and was given a prescription for medication.

After we left the doctor, Mr. Marvin wanted us to go and visit Aunt Jackie. I really didn't want to go because I didn't want to see her in the hospital bed looking helpless and what not. As we walked up to her room, things were exactly how I planned them in my head. Aunt Jackie was sitting up in bed with bandages wrapped around her hip and her head. She looked awful, but seemed to still be in good spirits.

"Here go my favorite boys that I've been waiting to see."

I think that Aunt Jackie forgot about everything that happened. Mr. Marvin walked over to her and gave her a kiss on her mouth as I just stood by the door and watched. I didn't want to go any closer to her because I didn't want to burst out in laughter or say something off, as they call it.

"Well baby, what happened with you?" Mr. Marvin asked as Aunt Jackie noticed me inching out the door.

"And where are you tryna go little boy?" Aunt Jackie caught me, but I didn't care.

"Oh, I was supposed to be taking Gina out to a comedy show tonight at Damond Gray's comedy lounge." I was hoping that they would still allow me to go because I needed this break.

"Did you talk to your Uncle and ask him if you could go?" Aunt Jackie asked as I looked over at Mr. Marvin as he began shaking his head.

"Uncle Marvin, can I please go?" I didn't know what else to do to get him to say yes because I knew I wasn't gonna beg him.

"I should say no and he knows why, but I'll let you go." Mr. Marvin smiled at me as Aunt Jackie kept asking him about what I did. I walked out of the room while reaching for my phone to call Gina.

"Hey wassup Gina baby?" I started chuckling as I heard her breathing on the other side of the phone.

"Hey daddy, so are we still on for tonight?" Gina still seemed interested and I was glad that she was.

Mr. Marvin let me use the car and said that he would catch a cab home so that I could enjoy myself tonight. Call me spoiled if you want, but I think I deserve it. Also, I think that they were allowing Aunt Jackie to go home because she had release forms on her stand, once they wrapped her hip and jaw. She had her clothes laying out on the chair next to her bed with crutches beside her clothes. I didn't want to question Mr. Marvin's decision, thinking about Aunt Jackie's discharge from the hospital. I jumped in the car and texted Patrick so that I could tell him about tonight. He responded by saying that it was weird that I was going on a date with his people's, but at the same time, he was for it. I knew that he would be though because we were just that tight and whatever decision I made, he always supported it.

It was 6:45 when I got home to get dressed. I took the quickest shower, but took my time oiling down my muscular body and ironing my clothes. I couldn't stop looking at myself in the mirror, winking at myself as I repeatedly looked back at the last text message from Gina that said she couldn't wait to spend time with me. By the time I got dressed and brushed my teeth, it was getting closer to 7:00. The comedy show was at 8:00 so I had just enough time to grab a bite to eat with her and chill until the show started. I got in the car and blasted my music to its highest level. Nothing or nobody else was on my mind, other than Gina and I didn't want anything to change my view about tonight.

I beeped my horn as I pulled up to Gina's crib, smiling from ear to ear, as I waited for her to strike the outside winds with her presence. Five minutes had gone by and there was still no sign of Gina. I texted her to inform her that I was sitting outside and she didn't respond; that was six minutes ago though. I started beeping the horn more intensely. Time was flying right past my eyes and the night wasn't getting any younger. My patience was running thin and I could feel my rage returning back into my body.

Gina finally decided to come out 15 minutes after I had been trying to get in touch with her. By the time we left and went on our way, it was 35 minutes after seven. I can't front though, although I was a little frustrated with this chick, my hormones started raging even more when she got in the car. I couldn't keep my eyes off of her and I knew that she knew I was horny. I planned for us to go to 'The Sutton's seafood spot' on Hazel Street, but because it was getting close to the time of the show, I had to readjust to something more quick.

"Daddy, so what you got planned for us tonight?"

I loved keeping secrets whenever I wanted to do something with a girl because I liked to see the reactions I would get from them.

"Chill ma, I got something special that I know you gonna love. I promise that this is only the beginning of something great." I started pouring out my emotions as I noticed Gina looking uninterested.

"I mean, I feel you daddy, just don't rush anything because remember, we are only friends." Gina reminded me as if I didn't know already.

Why is it that a girl always has to remind the dude of their status, like he doesn't know? Is it because that's the only way she can feel secure and protect her heart from any potential pain? These thoughts started to jump in my head and instead of respecting her for reminding me, like the average dude would, I responded the opposite.

"Look, maybe I need to stop calling you daddy because you seem to be taking things for a run and I don't want you catching feelings too fast, RJ." Gina continued talking and the more she talked, the more I grew sneakily angry.

"Aight, aight I got you ma. Imma just fall back and let you have ya way with this date. Just know, it's about to go down." I smiled as I rubbed my hand against her cheek.

I no longer felt the need to surprise her and take her to laugh at a comedy lounge, so I changed my plans altogether. About four minutes into our travel to the destination, the car remained quiet and I could feel awkward tension growing thick amongst us. The entire time I was driving, Gina was texting in her cell phone and it only made things worse. I pulled into an empty alley near Chestnut and Hazel Street, by the comedy lounge. While pulling into a little lot within the alley, I could tell the change on Gina's face.

"RJ, where are we at?" She kept asking as I continued to smile.

I turned the car off and took the keys out of the ignition as I leaned my car seat back to a tilt while looking into her eyes. My pipe was jumping and my muscles were starting to flex throughout my body. Before she could say another word, I quickly grabbed her mouth and placed my hand up her dress. My other hand started vibrating from her screams, but that motivated me even more to proceed. With one arm, I pulled her on my lap from the passenger seat while unzipping my jeans with the other hand. I never had the urge to do this type of thing before and I knew that there was no stopping now.

"Listen up! I better not hear that you said a word about this. Either you give it to me freely, or you let me take it freely. Imma try not to hurt you as much, but it depends on how much you cooperate with me." I started talking in my sexy voice as if I had been turning her on, but noticed that she was more afraid than anything as she looked at me with tears pouring onto my fingers.

Chapter Twenty Eight

June 29, 2008

It's been a week since the car accident and me being diagnosed with rapid eye movement syndrome. Me and Gina wasn't on good terms anymore, but it didn't bother me though because I had too much going on in my life. I started to feel like she was playing me anyway with all of those mixed signals she was giving me. (For future reference ladies, don't give dudes any mixed signals because it will catch up to you in the end). I tried calling Gina to apologize for our forced sexual session, but she won't answer my calls and I also know that she did exactly what I instructed her to do by not telling anybody. She kept that night between us because she knew what was in store for her if she didn't. Needless to say, Uncle Karl started coming around often since Aunt Jackie came home from the hospital. I thought that she would be coming home the same night of the accident, but I was a fool for even having those thoughts. Thinking that the forms on her stand was for her to be released from the hospital, I later found out that it was my prescription papers that Mr. Marvin must have slipped onto the stand when I wasn't looking so she could see them.

"Nephew come here so you can wash ya Aunt's hair." Uncle Karl yelled as I continued laying in the bed. Now why would this nigga have me washing Aunt Jackie's hair like I was a stylist or something?

"Aye Uncle Karl, that's for the birds!" I yelled back as I pulled the covers back onto my face.

Aunt Jackie was not disabled, but she always went into her childhood moods whenever Uncle Karl was around. Mr. Marvin was out getting a few groceries and afterwards, cleaning the church with the rest of the deacons. This bed that I was in was my place of happiness and I felt that when I left it, all of the happiness I once had was taken away from me. As I laid in my comfortable bed, looking around in the dark underneath my covers, I started to think about my life and where it had been taking me. The normal little church boy who once had all of the joy in the world and loved the company of his peers; that's not who I am any more. It's crazy how a child that's been raised in a Christian background is usually the main one's fighting and struggling with family secrets, sin, and everyday life. Shouldn't we be the one's to have complete access to freedom, especially if we're living right and doing all of the things that we should be doing?

I noticed in time that I was starting to loose my passion for loving God and depending on him to take control of my situations because he failed me every time I had the energy to call out his name. Satan him self seemed to fill in God's void of eagerness and came to the rescue just when I needed him the most. Satan even gave me advice and made his presence known to me, indicating that he was real and it really gave me great comfort. I'm not crazy; I just want to be loved and not have to look around for it. Enough of that because I don't want to scare you, so as I'm looking into the little bright star specs in darkness, my eyes grew heavy. Uncle Karl still continued trying to get my attention and I was surprised not to hear Aunt Jackie's voice, not one time. Being frustrated with it all, I instantly pulled the covers from over my eyes and seen that I was in the living room of my old house with my mom standing in the middle of the floor. She continued to look towards the front door as blood gushed in between her legs, like she was performing her own abortion or something. I tried walking over to her so that I could sit her down, but she didn't even notice my presence. That's when it hit me that this was all a dream. The ironic thing about it was that while I was sleep and dreaming, I realized none of this was real. I woke up still hearing Uncle Karl's voice, so I decided to finally go check ole man out and see what he wanted after putting my blade on the night stand.

"Did I or did I not tell ya ole' grumpy black ass to come down here so that you could wash your Aunt's hair?" Uncle Karl looked me dead in the eyes as he stood over Aunt Jackie.

"Uncle Karl for real though? Why are you making me do this?" I kept going on and on about how much this was for girls and I didn't get a good vibe by doing this.

"Negro, I don't care who you think it's for, but I know you better pick up that shampoo and that comb and get to work. I already set the warm water in the bucket for you to use."

Uncle Karl was determined to make me do this. Aunt Jackie just laid back on the reclining chair, silently laughing as I stood in back of her so that I could wash her hair. I couldn't believe that I was forced to do something that I didn't want to do, but I guess it was paybacks for doing what I did to Gina. I picked up the soaked sponge from inside of the bucket and squeezed the water onto Aunt Jackie's head. Uncle Karl seemed pleased by this because he aint say nothing the entire time he watched me.

"Boy you remind me so much of your mother and how she was stubborn, it don't make any sense." Uncle Karl proceeded in conversation.

"No, he reminds me a little of you too Uncle Karl, like the way you embrace and care for people, he get that from you and mom." Aunt Jackie added as she closed her eyes, enjoying the warm water touch her scalp. I just listened and waited to see where this was going as I picked up the bottle of shampoo.

"Do you know I had you all the time when you were an infant? Hell, I remember the time ya dad would bring you over to me because he needed lessons on changing your diapers." Uncle Karl started chuckling as Aunt Jackie joined him. We instantly started hearing keys making noise at the door and knew automatically that it was Mr. Marvin.

"How you doing Uncle Karl, Wassup baby, RJ?" Mr. Marvin greeted everyone else and when it came to me he only said my name. I knew that our relationship wasn't gonna get any better than it was. "I brought some spare ribs and vegetables, so I guess that's what we're having for dinner tonight." Mr. Marvin said as his voice echoed from the kitchen.

This day was so boring and a drag to me because all day, I had to help Uncle Karl with Aunt Jackie. It was 10:31 pm and I was over everything, including this day. None of my close friends were consistent any longer and I don't know where Lil Rodney had been. On the flip side of that, dinner was cool I guess you could say. Uncle Karl stayed around all day, but as soon as 9:00 pm hit, he grabbed his keys and was gone. Aunt Jackie seemed to enjoy his company though and I did too, surprisingly. I'm telling you, things seemed to start turning back into normal once I began taking two medicated pills each night. I was in a better mood and rarely had crazy dreams while I was sleep. I was afraid because I knew that tonight was going to be a little different than the other nights. I had run out of pills quickly, I guess because I took two each time I took naps throughout the day and before going to bed at night.

Uncle Karl and Uncle Marvin moved Aunt Jackie upstairs before Uncle Karl had left, so she ended her night early. Before I came upstairs, Mr. Marvin was downstairs working on a get well collage that he was putting together from his side of the family. Jaime was still over Ms. Connie's and I enjoyed every moment of the peace around the house while she was gone. I shut my door and jumped in bed, hoping that I could settle things with Gina in the morning when I got up. An hour later, something happened that I was not expecting to happen. Our house was being burglarized and I was hoping that Mr. Marvin settled everything before I got out of the bed, until I heard glass breaking and three loud gun shots. I couldn't move my body, but managed to draw my blade closer to me as I heard the foot steps coming up the stairs.

"Now, I'm not playing any more games with you or these people RJ!"

The voice sounded so familiar and crisp that I knew it was my dad.

"You havn't called me, or even tried getting my number from somebody!" My dad walked into my room with a TEC-9 in his hand.

"So you just gonna shoot me dad, you don't care nothing about my life because you've been gone for so long. Now you gonna try to come back and mend all the broken pieces that you disregarded?"

At this point I didn't want Aunt Jackie trying to get up out of the bed and put her nose in it because I was facing my fear after all.

"RJ I can't believe you right now son, here you are all messed up in the head and it's because of ya Aunt! She has poisoned ya innocent mind and captivated it with hidden motives that traveled throughout her family line!" My dad started walking closer to me.

"Aye yo pops, I'm not little no more so I would advise you to back off before this blade slice you into pieces!" I wasn't afraid of that gun because I knew he wouldn't use it.

"Lil nigga who you talking to boy?" My dad put the gun on the floor as he ran towards me, trying to ruff me up.

"Get off of me, I swear to God let me go!" I yelled from the top of my lungs and no longer cared who heard me.

"RJ... you really gonna stab me? RJJJJJJJJJJJJ", my dad started coughing up blood, just like Tim did as I continued jabbing my blade into his stomach.

"RJ, what's going on in there?" I could hear Aunt Jackie's crutches moving closer to the direction of my room as my dad continued wrestling with me.

"Oh my God..... Marvin", Aunt Jackie screamed as I noticed me standing up beside my bed in a pool full of blood.

"I was only tryna pray for him while he was sleeping', Mr. Marvin said as he took his last and final words. My life was over and I knew that there was no escaping this one. I began crying as I looked at Aunt Jackie drop to the floor, forgetting about her bruised hip; trying to breathe life back into Mr. Marvin. I ran downstairs so that I could grab some towels in the kitchen and noticed that Mr. Marvin had broken a glass cup when he was downstairs working on Aunt Jackie's collage earlier.

"Ahhhhhhhhhhhhhh Jesusssssssss", I heard Aunt Jackie screaming from the top of her lungs as I rushed back up the stairs to come to her rescue. As I got to the top step near my room, I fell down to the floor once I seen my blade inside Aunt Jackie's chest, near her heart.

"Auntie, Auntie what have I done to deserve this?", I began crying and yelling as I noticed Aunt Jackie still breathing.

"Nephew I can't take life anymore, especially without my husband. I prepared this nice long letter that I wanted to talk over with you once you read it. It seems that everything happened entirely too soon and now you gotta figure things out without me. Isn't that what you wanted and what Ray and everybody else wanted as well?" Aunt Jackie said as she punched the blade deeper into her chest, causing her to completely loose her life line. I picked up the letter and noticed pictures falling from her night gown that she had on. Without thinking twice, I quickly grabbed all that I could and put it in Mr. Marvin's car. I snatched the letter with the pictures, shut my bedroom door and without thinking, quickly made an escape for it before the sun began to raise above the morning skies.

Chapter Twenty Nine

The next day got even worse and I came to the conclusion that life was no longer the same for me anymore. My world turned upside down and my depressive state went into effect instantly. I had no one to turn to or confide in any longer because my thinking was all messed up. I could no longer find trust in other people, only neglect from people. I never thought I would find myself in this predicament, especially since I was involved in church and came from a Christian family. Funny thing is that no matter how much Aunt Jackie preached to me about being the chosen one or even being special, I never would believe it and by her current actions, it just showed me that she didn't either; Her faith was haunted by fear and overshadowed with doubt. I felt so low today and didn't have any inspiration to see the reality of things for what they really were. At this point, I was scared to move on into a fruitful future, so I decided to just chill in the past.

Today was Friday June 20th, 2008 and it was 8:23 in the morning. I couldn't believe all of that stuff just happened, especially the fact of Aunt Jackie making a great impact on my life forever. Her words no longer meant nothing as I pondered on all of the things that she told me once before. I parked in a vacant abandoned warehouse on the other side of town where all of the Hispanics lived. I figured that I would hide out until I came to the acceptance of everything that happened from the night before. *Ring... Ring... Ring... Ring*

My phone had been ringing non stop and I was confused to see my house number being read on the screen. I was too scared to pick it up because nobody was there during the time of the accident, so I turned off my phone and broke it into two pieces. As I looked on the passenger's seat, I seen a lot of stuff that I collected before I headed out of the house last night. I picked up all of the pictures and scanned through them once again, discovering a picture that I didn't see once before of Uncle Karl and my mom with me in her arms when she was in the hospital. Because I was aggravated and disturbed by this picture, I ripped it up and threw it out of the window of the car and onto the concrete ground. I then picked up the long handwritten letter from Aunt Jackie that she had been telling me about before she took her last breath.

03-08-2008
To my nephew Raven Hill,

I would like to start off by saying that you have always been one to carry on the strength of the family, even when you didn't know that you were. There are a lot of things that we haven't covered yet and it saddens me to know that we never will because of the fear of conviction I have at this present moment. I prepared this letter for you just to avoid verbally telling you how I was feeling. I'm not an expert in holding family secrets because there are a lot of things that comes with it, including doubt to think that one will never get over whatever was done to them. I know that by writing you this letter and getting everything off of my chest, this will be the only way that I gain my freedom and deliverance back. When I was a child growing up around 15 years old, I never had anyone close that I considered trust worthy because all of my friends stabbed me in the back one way or another. The only people that I had, was your mother and Uncle Karl. I promise you this, Uncle Karl was one that me and your mother poured out so much to because he was the only one that presented understanding when it came to certain issues that we both were dealing with. When our mother died a little before I started tenth grade, things changed and my life had been considered a lie because I had to live with the thought of a sexual experience that me, your mother and Uncle Karl had all at once. Uncle Karl forced me and your mother into a threesome with him after we moved in with him. He would sit us on the bed, introducing us to adult flicks as he poured lotion into our hands with a smile. We had no other choice but to go on with it because we didn't know the consequences of what he would do to us. He would repeat these habits for months and years up until we turned 18. Around this time, your mother had just hooked up with your father Brandon, so it was much easier for her to run to someone in times of trouble. When it came to me, I had no one to turn to except Uncle Karl, however each moment that we spent more time with each other after the days and weeks passed, he seemed to cease his sexual desires and chase those thoughts away from us because he wanted to gain a normal relationship back again with us, I guess.

A month after our last sexual adventure with Uncle Karl, your mother came to me and told me that she was pregnant. I didn't know what to think about it because before our encounter with Uncle Karl, she had just lost her virginity to your father. I told her not to say anything to either one of them and to wait until you were born. Your father Brandon had just went forth with adopting your brother, little Brandon and that entire process because he told her that he didn't think he could have children and to be honest, I really don't know why they were considering any at that time. Anyway, so by sharing this foolishness, it would have gotten in the way of things.

Nine months later, you were born and by this time it still wasn't out that we shared a sexual experience with Uncle Karl to your father. Things started to reveal itself for what it was worth the day of Halloween, five years after. I couldn't believe that we held all of this for five years and to be honest I thought that it would never get out because we had been holding it for so long. Anyway, the day of Halloween, your father had been laid off from his job because he was caught stealing money from the safe just so that he could provide for the family. The money that he was getting from the state for Brandon wasn't really cutting it for him so he did what he had to do and in result paid the consequences for it. He walked into the house while me and your mother were in the dining room ironing you and Brandon's ninja costumes. We didn't notice him walking into the house, but once we heard him, we looked back to the direction of the door. He had a piece of paper in his hands and looked mad as ever. The day before, your mother took Uncle Karl to get a DNA test and it came back negative, just like Brandon's results. Brandon was disgusted and pissed by this and that's what caused the argument that you and little Brandon witnessed when you guys came in from school that evening. I was thrown for a loop as well because I was confident you're your mother didn't have many sexual partners, especially since she was involved with Brandon. Uncle Karl was shocked by this because he knew that he would have to live with the guilt. Big Brandon threatened that he would send little Brandon back with the state and get the last check for taking care of him. I was at a lost for words because I was stuck in the middle of all of this, but I will say that he didn't put his hands on her because it would have been a done deal for him. As he went to get Brandon from up stairs, I had witnessed your mother having a seizure and heart attack at the same time. They run heavy in our family and to tell you the truth, that's what killed our father. Tears filled my eyes and I fell to the floor to catch her from hitting her head and just as I was doing that, I ran to the front room because I heard crying and stomping coming from the steps. I allowed little Brandon to go with your father because he had all legal rights and I didn't. The only thing that I could do was protect you and make sure that you were safe because your mother had all legal rights over you. You were officially considered *the only child that your mother ever had, but I tried to do everything that I could to make things comfortable for you. I would always sing a song that my mother sung in times of trouble because it soothed me in a way that I had never felt before. Your father was later arrested for getting caught up in a drug bust that I previously warned the cops about.*

After your mother's death, I tried keeping in contact with him so that he could have time with you, but it didn't work out. Fear always haunted me because I knew that Brandon would one day get out and retaliate on what I did to him. My relationship with Uncle Karl was no more and I couldn't really figure out why. When your father was finally released, he threatened to tell you the truth about everything and bring harm to the family. I didn't think that you were old enough to hear all of that because it would have been too overwhelming for you to take all of it in at one time. I didn't meet Ray until later on after me and your father agreed to establish some mutual agreements over lunch. Your father had Ray with him, but I guess he used him as a witness, just for safety with the law. I never trusted Ray though because of the looks that he gave me and it shocked me once I knew that he was hanging with little Rodney. I thought that I got over those feelings, but they seemed to never let go. I said all of this to say that truth is better said then being discovered because in the end, it will remain what it is; true. I never meant to hold this from you and cause even more hurt to our family. Living with this has definitely put me in a place of unhappiness and guilt. Happy Birthday!!!,

Aunt Jackie

I couldn't believe that I was fatherless and that Aunt Jackie and my mom had a threesome with Uncle Karl. Aunt Jackie wanted to present this letter to me on my birthday, but I guess she extended the time a little longer. More hate towards Uncle Karl started to form inside of me because although things were the way they were, he was nonchalant. I wanted to take action and run up in his house and puncture his lungs with my foot, but I started to realize that I no longer had the energy to. I put the key back into the ignition and started to pull out of the abandoned warehouse. It was now 11:10 am and I was ready to head back to the reality of things and face all of the things that I couldn't before. As I drove in Uncle Marvin's car, thoughts of anger hit me once more as I continued doing 95 on the highway on my way back to the house.

'I'm ready for whatever, even if this is the end of me.' I said to myself as tears poured from my eyes. I no longer had the energy to retaliate and have people imagining how I was feeling. As I pulled back into the development of my house, butterflies started to hit my stomach as a form of shame came to mind. I looked over at Lil Rodney's crib and seen that his door was open. I parked in front of the house as I seen him coming out of the house.

"Aye RJ, the undertaker's just came to your house and took two body bags away. What happened yo?" Lil Rodney asked.

"Nothing Rodney, nothing."

"Yo ya peoples on ya dad side just called my crib and told me that Ray killed himself in the pin yo. They said that he suffered great depression and was on suicidal watch for like three days. It seems like everybody going through it and I don't know who to turn to with my issues and problems." Lil Rodney started crying as tears filled my eyes.

"Man this world aint for me, it aint for none of us!"

I left Lil Rodney outside with the rest of the nosy neighbors that I could see looking through their windows at me.

I rushed inside of the house to grab a few more things, including money from Mr. Marvin's safe that he held in him and Aunt Jackie's room. When I opened the door, I noticed it looked the same way it did the night before. It had caution tape on the outside of the house, but I still proceeded to come in. I wanted to get in and out of the house as quickly as I could, so I didn't waste any time grabbing what I needed. From the top of the stairs I could see that my room had a chalk sketch of Aunt Jackie and Mr. Marvin with caution tape at the door. I tried my best not to step on the chalk. I didn't know when or if the police were coming back so I didn't want to disturb the crime scene and I definitely didn't want to be there if they came back. As I opened the front door to leave out the house, I saw Uncle Karl's car pull into the driveway.

Chapter Thirty

As I closed the front door behind me, I tucked a piece of glass in my hand. Uncle Karl got out of his car and started yelling at me. I had tuned him out though so I don't even know what he was saying. When he got close enough, I hooked the glass across the face of the man I discovered to be a liar, insincere, visionless and distorted pain.

"Ahhhhhhhh you black cuss, I'm calling the cops on your dysfunctional ass!" Uncle Karl yelled out as he covered his face with his hand.

"I can't believe that you would allow Aunt Jackie to hold such a secret about what you did to her and my mom. Homie, you will never be apart of me and you wont start now!"

I forced my foot in his chest as he fell back into the grass. "That's for my mom and Aunt Jackie!" I walked up to him with a smile as I ran back in the house to grab the gasoline lighter fluid from the basement.

"Your gonna pay for this young man, as long as God is my witness, you will reap what you sow!"

Uncle Karl kept talking his talk as he laid helplessly on the lawn, still covering his face up. I went down into the basement and seen all of my old school stuff from the time that I was a kid in kindergarten and started chuckling when I seen a picture of me and Brandon when we were on the playground. I grabbed the picture and the fresh can of gasoline fluid, running back out of the house.

"Aye Uncle Karl, I want you to visualize a kid in the middle of an empty world where he is surrounded by terror and fear as he tries to find his way to safety." I said as I took the top off from the gasoline can. "That young boy has been me for the past 18 years of my life and it's sad that even when you had the chance to free me from the demise of misery, you stood over me, knowing the truth while laughing and sipping on some gin. Now I want you to think about something else Uncle Karl. *Imagine Me!*"

    I poured the gasoline onto his head as I pulled a lighter out from my pocket. Without thinking about my actions, I lit the match and released it onto the top of his head. I watched as he screamed for help as his head lit on fire. I started laughing because it looked like something from in a movie. Uncle Karl was loud enough for the neighbors to hear him and to be honest; I didn't care because I wanted to him to suffer just like I had been doing for years. I started to make a run to my car as I saw the neighbors coming out of their houses.

    I jumped in the car and drove off with Lil Rodney standing in the middle of the street as I noticed the neighbors running with buckets of water to put out the fire. From a distance, I saw Pastor Clay driving up into our development and another deacon from our church. Pastor Clay noticed Mr. Marvin's car and turned his car around to follow me. I tried shaking him up when I got in the car, but he wouldn't allow me to. I don't know how the church people found out about this stuff, but just like all church people, those niggas nosy. I rode around town before I made an escape into the winds as I started crying uncontrollably. My life, my family and my friends could have been extremely better if I knew what I knew a while ago. I don't think things would be the same if these secrets came out earlier in the game.

    It was now 3:05 in the afternoon and I went back into my dungeon at the abandoned warehouse on the other side of town. I think I lost Pastor Clay once I cut through cars and switched lanes like crazy. My entire body started to shake and my heart began racing as I pulled out Aunt Jackie pills from the glove department that she always left inside of the car. I knew that this moment would be the end of me because everybody that I loved, including my long lost dad was out of my life forever and a day. I blasted the music as I leaned my seat back, just so that I could relax. As I started to get in the groove of the music, I pulled out some pills from the bottle and popped them into my mouth. Closing my eyes and thinking about my life as a whole, I swallowed each pill one by one while laying back into my seat as the music took me away. "I wish everything was all a dream." I said as my vision began getting blurry and my heart started slowing down. My eyes began to get dimmer and the sound of the music began to fade away. I knew that at this very moment, my life has been imagined by you. THE END!!!

After reading of much strife that I never knew RJ had been experiencing within himself, I closed the journal instantly. Today was August 23rd, 2008 and I noticed that his last date was marked two months ago. I rushed to the only hospital in town after Pastor Clay informed me about RJ. On my way to the hospital, it blew me to see how much of a bad person I was made out to be, when in fact I was actually the good guy. I never had the chance to express my emotions and feelings because I wasn't given the opportunity. As I sat in the waiting room to find out if RJ made it through, I looked at the picture left in the journal by RJ of him and little Brandon. I don't know how and why, but Pastor Clay got Lil Rodney to give me this journal a month ago. I started realizing how much the stories in his journal full of pain, confusion and tragedy had made an impact on me.

"Mr. Brandon Z. Hill, are you ready to hear this."

The doctor said as she walked over to me with papers in her hands. "I have some good news and some bad news to give you." I was nervous as crap, but I knew that I had to get myself together. "We have the reports of Raven Hill. I regret to inform you that Mr. Raven Hill did not make it, due to an overdose he had. Good news is that the medical examiners faxed us his autopsy for you to see with additional information, however the bad news is that the state ruled that his body be cremated since no one came to identify him in time. The interesting thing about this is that it's been recently discovered that Raven Hill's biological father's last name is Droppins. As we investigated this, case workers stated that Raven's mother didn't want Droppins on the birth certificate after he signed it. It was too late and because of the time she told us, we couldn't do anything about it. Apparently Mr. Droppins has been involved in a series of fraudulent investigations that go back fifteen years. He should have been arrested years ago, but because he changed up his identity, it was hard to find him in the system. His wife recently filed a divorce and exposed him to the police, giving them the alias name, Clay. Once they heard this, they quickly shipped this information to investigators, who then scanned the information. He was a smart guy, he opened a church up in her name and houses and cars as well, but made sure it was under her maiden name. There is still a search out for him, but as far as Mr. Raven Hill, he was sent to the morgue last month and was cremated. Luckily your name and information was listed as Jackie Jones's emergency contact, but after trying to reach you for so long, it was too late. If you need anything, we offer counseling as well as other things to assist you in coping with all of this."

The doctor rubbed my back as I put my head down with so much tears in my eyes. My son, Raven Hill had committed suicide and died with the thought of life being some bad place, not even considering the great things about it. I know that things will never be the same and no matter how much I try to erase the negative thoughts of tragedy, I cant. I wish that I was around RJ more to let him know that everything would be alright, but when I think more into the situation; there was nothing else that I could do. I couldn't believe that this man, who went by Pastor Clay for years, had been neglecting his kid, Raven. I can't believe this nigga was leading a church and living the good life, while Jackie and the rest of the crew was left confused, trying to figure out life. Just like RJ, everything and I mean everything had been taken away from me and the only place that I could go to in times of trouble were the streets. I knew that by doing this, I would get all of the comfort that I needed and I could start a new life in memory of my old one.

While holding the autopsy report in my hand, all I could do was smile and walk away. I made a quick call to my home boy Pops from the hood, over in Holland's Place and was bout to get this business on a roll. While waiting for Pops to come through on the line, I started laughing as I thought about RJ and his infamous line. "Nah, I can't be the good guy no more because it aint worth it, now take that and *Imagine ME!*"

Autopsy Report of Raven Hill

Office of Chief Medical Examiner

Mercy Medical Examiner's District

Thaton County

125 Goodman Rd, Thaton County 35241-2525

(198) 526-9845 Fax: (198) 236-2546

Autopsy Report

Name: Raven Hill

Case No: 651102IU

Approximate Age: 18 years

Height: 63 inches

Weight: 175.5 pounds

Sex: Male

We hereby certify that on the ninth day of June 20 2008, pursuant to Statute 56.20 of Thaton County Criminal Code, an autopsy on the body of Raven Hill was performed at the Mercy Medical Examiner's Office in Thaton County and upon investigation of the essential facts concerning the circumstances of the death and history of the case, we are of the opinion that the cause of death was as follows:

FINDINGS:
　I.　Sudden death associated with:
　　　a.　(RBD) - Rapid Eye Movement Behavior Disorder:

            i. Fully blown was diagnosed in 2008.
            ii. Third stage
    b. Found in his abdomen Buspirone
    c. Postmortem toxicology:
            i. Cardiac blood fluoxetine= 5.26 ug/ml
            ii. Femoral vein blood fluoxetine= 0.2365 ug/ml
            iii. Gastric fluoxetine= 9.6 ug/ml
            iv. Liver fluoxetine= 59.23 ug/ml
    d. Postmortem blood 50 heavy metal screen negative
    e. Postmortem blood mercury negative (above average detection level)

COMMENT:
Raven Hill was 18 years of age at the time of his death. He was in a 2004 s500 Mercedes Benz convertible parked in a Morris and Chestnut Warehouse in Thaton County. Victim was found in the car with a pill bottle of Buspirone in his hand. When the Police department arrived at the scene, victim was unresponsive and appeared to be dead for an approximate day or two (36 - 48 hours). The Medical examiner from Mercy Hospital was contacted and came and retrieved the body. He was pronounced dead on site at 2:50pm on June 23, 2008.

Records obtained from Greater Medical Center in Thaton County indicated that Mr. Hill was previously diagnosed with Rapid Eye Movement Behavior Disorder.

Mr. Hill prescribed Ambien CR pills.

Rapid Eye Movement Behavior Disorder is a disorder that causes a person to respond to dramatic or violent dreams during the REM stage sleep. The autopsy revealed cuts and bruises on his hand which could have possibly come from hurting himself while in the act of the REM stage sleep.

The pill bottle later discovered in his hand during the time of his death was Buspirone and was identified to be prescribe to 39 year old, Jackie Jones of Thaton County.

Cause of Death: Overdose to Anxiety medication also known as Buspirone.

Manner of Death: Suicide

Signature: Gary D. Brown, M.D.

Signature: Kendell M. Farkes, M.D.

A CERTIFIED COPY ATTEST JUNE 25, 2008 Kendell M. Farkes, M.D. CHIEF MEDICAL EXAMINER Thaton County BY [signature] Charles

White

Author Acknowledgments

Writing this novel has been such an exciting journey that I can never take back. I personally believe that the ministry and life that came from out of this book will touch many homes, inside and out, mend the broken, heal the lost and fill in the voids of true love from a family. Not often, we the people experience true support and admiration towards any goals or dreams from those we seek it from. But first, I must give recognition and say that I am extremely humbled and appreciative for YOU, the reader. Your purchase lets me know that you support my zeal to progress in the direction of success and act on any aspirations that I may have.

I also want to give reference and give many thanks to my #1 who has paved the way, enabled me with favor and activated my gifts, **God, my heavenly father**. By taking this step in writing this novel and also presenting who you are to the people, I pray that you are pleased with me. I LOVE YOU with ALL of me, thanks for your support and love pops.

To my guiding light and my heart, the legendary **Pastor Louvenia Dickerson**. Pastor, it's because of you that I have learned how to embrace the manifestation of promise. Your wisdom, strength and love throughout the years has enabled me access to be all that I can be. Your life and all that you stand for has inspired, motivated and encouraged me in many ways that I could not begin to make mention of. Your legend and all that you have imparted here on earth to many people will always live in me. Thank you and I LOVE YOU!!

To my precious lamb, my God Daughter **Jordyn**. There's not a day that goes by that I don't appreciate God for you. One that is full of life and energy, you keep me going. God daddy loves you sweetheart and wants you to know that you will never have to ask for anything in life, but rather enjoy the essence and the benefits from it. LOVE YOU JoJo!!!

To my most prized possessions, my parents **Danielle & Anthony Walker Sr.** You have taught me so much in life, starting at an early age and because of your dedication to nurture with great wisdom and push for originality and integrity, I am who I am today. You both are the beats to my heart and I am grateful that you have lived this moment to witness such a movement. Thank you for your sacrifices throughout the years and for your consistency of making sure that I will never be a day without. LOVE YOU FOREVER!!!

To my other half, my little brother ***Antwone***. Growing up, mom and dad would often ask us what we wanted to be and you were certain that you would be a drummer boy, just as I would respond to being a singer. Sometimes I sit back and laugh because I never imagined writing a book, yet I am an author and now you want to pursue your rapping career. You are one that I will always hold close to my heart, although you may get on my nerves at times. But hey, that's a little brother for ya'! I pray that I haven't failed you at being the big brother you've always wanted. You are MY success and the reason why my drive to succeed is so strong. I LOVE YOU little Bro!!!

To my Backbone, my grandmother ***Elease "Sally" Hawkins***. You exemplify, coming from my eyes what LOVE really is. Out of all the things I've learned and experienced in life, you have taught me how to embrace and operate in love. You're my jewel and the reason that I live with passion. I LOVE YOU *Sista' Sal.*

To my Joy & the melody to my song, my aunt ***Tara Williams***. I can't begin to thank you for being the person you are to me. You have given me much security and understand the man I'm becoming. You are of great value to my life auntie, considering the fact that you're my outlet and listening ear (Little things matter the most). I love you for the qualities you present to life and appreciate your encouragement to be different. I LOVE YOU!!!

To my guardian angel, my little cousin ***Willie "Brian" Williams III***. You rock lil' man! I remember the tender years of your infant days, you would always cry when someone other than I picked you up. I'm proud of the young man you're becoming and am happy that we have crossed paths, here on earth as family. You survived the worst of times from your sickness of being diagnosed with sickle cell and I'm completely grateful that you're an over comer. Keep striving to be fearfully and wonderfully made in the image of God and you will go far. My hero, my motivator, my mini me, *Brian* your simply my inspiration. You crushed on the book cover and other promotional ads for the book. Job well done, thank you! I LOVE YOU ALWAYS lil' man.

To my *Family*, I personally want you all to know that I am raising the bar for us all. I appreciate the individual relationships I have with all of you and the experiences we're continuing in life together. As long as I have, YOU will always have. My dream in life has always been to place our family's legacy on a platform of greatness and with your dedication to support, WE DID IT! Thanks for being my #1 supporters and loving/protecting me HARD. This is just the beginning for us. I LOVE YOU ALL!!!

To my Church Family, **Conquering Power Church of Deliverance**. You all have a special place in my heart and I'm extremely grateful for our ministry and what we present to the world thus far. *Pastor Hayward R. Hamilton & Lady Tamara Hamilton*, through many things, I know that I can depend on you guys for the love, support, protection and encouragement that you present me with. Your efforts to assist and provide for me will never be overlooked by shame, but rather visually enhanced with thankfulness. Let's go higher and EMERGE. I LOVE YOU ALL!!! #TeamConquer

To my Ace Boon Coons, Best friends, and Brother's forever **Melvin & Darrell.** I am privileged to have you both be apart of my life, from the times you both came into my life. As a little boy, it was always my prayer to have a best friend that I would be able to share and experience venues in life with. Not only did he fulfill what I requested, but he provided me with two. *Mel*, you are really my twin brother, sometimes I think you were long lost and connected back up with me, Ha! Through many situations, you've always been my inspiration and I thank you. *Rell*, I'm so grateful to experience such a friendship with you. I've learned many things regarding friendships from the time I met you and can appreciate everything that you have imparted. You both hold great value to my life. Thanks for putting up with me fellas!!! My best friends, your still here and I LOVE YOU.

To the TWO BEST organizations that Virginia State University could ever offer on campus, my family the *Virginia State University Gospel Chorale (VSUGC) & People Against Negativity Inspiring Creativity (P.A.N.I.C 2000)*. My experience at Virginia State would mean nothing if I didn't consider being apart of such great movements. *VSUGC*, I want to thank ALL of you for your prayers, dedication, support and love. To the advisor of the choir, *Dr. James Holden (Pop Holden)* thanks for everything, literally. You definitely have played a major part in my life and have taken the initiative to consider me as your own. I really appreciate the individual relationships I hold with each of you. Special shout out to my VSUGC male quartet brothers. #VSUGCcccceee! *P.A.N.I.C 2000*, you all have motivated me to pursue my career in such a way that I can't even start to put in words. In being apart of such a distinct, yet amazing performing organization, I have learned, experienced and grasped true dedication, perseverance and DRIVE. I really appreciate everything you all presented me with and will never take back the investment of love you all provided me with. Special Shout out to my coming in line, *Fall2k10 'Generation X'*. I couldn't have gone through many experiences without ALL OF YOU! I hold you all very close to me and will always remember every moment we spent together. Special shout out to our momma, *Breanna Goodwin*. I appreciate the person you are and everything you stand for. P.A.N.I.C, remember we win at the end of the day because it's extremely obvious that WE JUST DON'T DANCE, WE PERFORM!!! #OooooooooooohhhhOoooooooooh. Both families, I LOVE YOU!!!

Born in Wilmington, Delaware, Anthony D. Walker Jr. comes from a city where talent is scarce, crime emerges, and history-making young people are hidden behind a desolate future.

In 2008, Walker left the City of Wilmington to pursue higher education at the Virginia State University, where he is currently studying Mass Communications, with great future plans to construct and open his very own production studio. Facing both individuality and adversity, Walker is reminded of a famous quote written by Frederick Douglass: "Without struggle there can be no progress."

Walker has always been known to have a strong passion for his generation and his hometown. Growing up in the project homes on Locust Street, also known as "The Bucket" on the north side of Wilmington, Walker, a 20 year old Visionary wants to do whatever it takes make an impact on his community and make the people who have watched his growth since infancy very proud of his personal achievement.

Even in his childhood and teenage years, Walker has always been a unique child that showed much interest in acting and entertainment. "This was always something that caught my eye, whether on field trips in school or in a movie. As I entered my teen years, I formed an entertainment group called 'Krazy Kidz' that consisted of my family. During this time, I would compose story lines, produce and direct them, then later film it on my little camcorder. I can certainly laugh about it now, but ultimately that is what pushed me into pursuing my career in the entertainment industry." says Walker, reminiscing his childhood entertainment adventures.

Walker is not only known as a 21st Century Author, but has notably been recognized as a successful and skilled Model, Actor, and Singer. Giving in to his other unique and passionate talents, Walker has appeared in several noted fashion and entertainment productions. To name a few, he has appeared in "Models in Wonderland", hosted by the Alpha Phi Alpha Fraternity Inc, "The Gospel According to Fashion" hosted by Cameron Washington Enterprises, and has written and directed his first stage play, "A Christmas Desire", hosted by the Drama Department of Conquering Power Church of Deliverance.

Through psychological thinking and realistic nature of rarely touched storylines and hidden truths, "Imagine Me" is as a Christian-based novel written to stimulate your mind and emotions as it takes you through the journey of a young boy who over the important moments in time, finds out what really defines him and what he has become.

In reflecting over the novel Walker says, "The title speaks for itself as you can see. I never thought that the story line would consist of so much distress regarding situations concerning family, yet it makes sense because there are many obstacles in which individuals find hard to defeat regarding generational curses." With the motivation and drive to educate and bring awareness to individual homes and families, Walker's mission through this novel is to reintroduce the principle of transparency, support, and love to this generation.

The destiny and future success that awaits this young author is inevitable. Endowed with knowledge and undeniable wisdom, Walker is bound to make such an implosion in the literacy community. After Grad School, Walker plans to continue making preparations and final decisions to establish and CEO his very own production studio, "Walker-To-Walker Entertainment".

The Multi-talented Walker also desires to also establish a foundation for youth across the entire United States, who have many aspirations and have a desire and motivation to pursue their dreams and perfect their individual talents in the entertainment industry.

Walker aspires to pave the way for this generation and those to come, encouraging them to go after whatever they imagined would never come into existence, pushing his personal motivation quote "Activating the Gifts in ME."

www.ingramcontent.com/pod-product-compliance
Lightning Source LLC
Chambersburg PA
CBHW032043150426
43194CB00006B/400